10/06

"Look at Mickey Mouse./Look at Minnie Mouse./
They just live on love and chee-eeze."—Lyric from the Mack Gordon–Harry Revel song
"It's the Animal in Me" sung by Ethel Merman in the Paramount film *The Big Broadcast of 1936*

MICKEY

THE EVOLUTION, THE LEGEND,

BY ROBERT HEIDE **AND** JOHN GILMAN
WITH MONIQUE PETERSON **AND** PATRICK WHITE

A WELCOME BOOK

EDITIONS

NEW YORK

MOUSE
THE PHENOMENON!

For information address Disney Editions,
114 Fifth Avenue, New York, NY 10011-5690.
Editorial Director: Wendy Lefkon
Senior Editor: Sara Baysinger
Copy Chief: Monica Mayper
Senior Copyeditor: Christopher Caines
Associate Editor: Jody Revenson

Produced by Welcome Enterprises, Inc.,
588 Broadway, New York, NY 10012.
Project Director: H. Clark Wakabayashi
Project Manager: Jacinta O'Halloran
Designer: Jon Glick

Printed in Canada
First Edition
10 9 8 7 6 5 4 3 2 1

Library of Congress Cataloging-in-Publication Data
on file.
ISBN: 0-7868-5353-0

Visit www.disneyeditions.com

FRONTISPIECE: *A record-breaker at
auction, the highly prized windup
toy manufactured by the Tipp
Company of Germany features
Mickey and Minnie on a motorcycle.*

TITLE PAGE: Storybook illustration
from The Adventures of Mickey
Mouse Book #1, published in
1931 by David McKay, New York.

TABLE OF CONTENTS

INTRODUCTION: AN EXCEPTIONAL MOUSE TALE ... 6

CHAPTER 1: AN UNLIKELY HERO ... 12
  THE BIG BANG ... 15
  SQUARE-SHOOTING MICKEY MICE ... 22
  A MOUSE FOR ALL MERCHANTS ... 29
  TOAST OF THE TOWN ... 36
  ROLE-MODEL MICKEY ... 48

CHAPTER 2: CITIZEN MICKEY ... 58
  MAN OR MOUSE? ... 60
  THE SORCERER'S APPRENTICE ... 66
  ON THE HOME FRONT ... 73

CHAPTER 3: THE COMEBACK KID ... 88
  TRAP TIME ... 90
  MOUSE IN THE HOUSE ... 94
  A WALK IN THE PARK ... 106

CHAPTER 4: COUNTERCULTURAL POP STAR ... 112
  PEACE, LOVE, AND MICKEY ... 115
  FLEA-MARKET MICKEY ... 120
  MICKEY REVIVAL ... 126
  SUPERSTAR STATUS ... 136
  BIRTHDAY BOY ... 142

CHAPTER 5: THE BIG CHEESE ... 148
  RENAISSANCE MOUSE ... 151
  THE WORKS ... 158
  THE SHOW MUST GO ON ... 165

AFTERWORD: LOVE, MICKEY ... 177
MICKEY MOUSE FILMOGRAPHY ... 186
SELECTED BIBLIOGRAPHY ... 188
INDEX ... 189
ACKNOWLEDGMENTS ... 192

Mickey Mouse: A Walt Disney animated cartoon character so universally known as to have entered into American popular culture folklore, Mickey debuted in "Steamboat Willie" (1928), the first animated cartoon with sound.

—excerpt from an entry in *The Penguin Dictionary of American Folklore* (2000), by Alan Axelrod and Harry Oster

Mickey Mouse's life is a story of rags to riches if ever there was one. His rise to greatness proves the American Dream is possible, even for a little cartoon character. When Mickey Mouse was first introduced to the American public at the end of the Jazz Age, he proved to be both memorable and loveable. His antics mirrored those of popular film stars of the day, and his imagination and bravery appealed to ordinary Americans eager to cheer for the victories of the underdog. The circumstances of Mickey's birth brought together the ingredients necessary for success: the advent of sound in film made it possible for Mickey to move in time to playful melodies, to squeal and shriek, and eventually to speak; the graphic arrangement of rounded forms that Ub Iwerks first penned had an indubitable appeal; and Mickey's unshakeable and undefeatable optimism met a world-weary public eager to receive him into their hearts. This powerful combination gave Mickey an irresistible allure.

The humble circumstances of Mickey's birth gave no inkling of the stardom that he would eventually achieve. In 1926, the twenty-seven-year-old Disney had fallen victim to his own naïveté about the legal affairs of the film industry. He had unwittingly signed a contract that gave up his rights to Oswald the Lucky Rabbit, the star character developed by his associate, leading animator, and longtime friend, Ub Iwerks. On the heels of this disaster, Walt asked Ub to create a new character that the Disney Brothers Cartoon Studios could promote as its own. A panel of cartoon animals by Meeker that Ub found in a magazine gave him the idea for a mouse character. It seemed like an original idea—the only mouse in cartoons at the time was Krazy Kat's sidekick, Ignatz. An old publicity photo of Walt

6

OPPOSITE: *Pyrotechnics over Cinderella Castle in Walt Disney World, Florida, create a radiant backdrop for the Partners sculpture, portraying Walt Disney and Mickey Mouse.*

surrounded by mice drawn by Hugh Hartman also influenced Mickey's design, as did memories of a real mouse that that had climbed up on Walt's drawing board when he was a young animator in Kansas City. Walt had befriended the little creature, named him Mortimer, and trained him to accept tidbits from his hand. Walt proposed the name Mortimer for Ub's new character, too, but the moniker didn't seem to suit Ub's snappy design. It was Walt's wife, Lillian, who suggested the name Mickey. Mickey Mouse—it sounded right. Together, Ub and Walt set out to create Mickey's personality and make his first cartoons.

In developing Mickey's personality, Walt drew on the enduring American values of optimism, self-reliance, and courage. Mickey embodies the enterprising spirit of the country at the time he was born. From the start, he related to everyman worries and concerns, and his keen ability to get himself out of trouble or tight situations was uplifting. There wasn't an area of American life that Mickey didn't traverse. He was a superb impersonator of celebrated Americans from Charles Lindbergh and Charlie Chaplin to Douglas Fairbanks and Jimmy Durante. Unlike many Hollywood stars who are typecast in specific roles, Mickey could do it all and he did it well. He was a musician, a magician, a conductor, a bandleader, a dancer, a boatbuilder, a pilot, a hunter, a Romeo, a giant slayer, a hotdog vendor, a policeman, a plumber, a fireman, a football player, an Olympian, a detective, a cowboy, an inventor, and a family man. He crossed over into myriad genres, including musicals, westerns, romantic comedies, and thrillers, without compromising his core identity.

Mickey draws people to him. He connects with his audiences, and they welcome him with open arms. People look at Mickey and see themselves; they see something familiar embodied in his gestures. He makes them laugh, and feel joy and compassion. He even makes them love him.

Like the composite figure described by mythographer Joseph Campbell in his seminal 1949 book, *The Hero with a Thousand Faces*—albeit on a smaller, mouse-sized scale—Mickey exemplifies the archetypal hero celebrated in diverse cultures worldwide. In story after story, Mickey prevails in trials that test his courage, his ingenuity, and his faith in himself. Although he emerged, not from the dark precincts of folklore or legend, but in the spotlit arena of popular commercial entertainment, the Mouse shares many features with the protagonists of the great myths. It is his mythical resonance that perhaps best explains Mickey's enduring appeal, and the ease with which he has moved beyond animated cartoons to every available genre and medium.

When Mickey's career in Hollywood started to wane, he found a home in the new medium of television. In the 1950s, he hosted the *Mickey Mouse Club* and the *Wonderful World of Color*. Mickey introduced his audience to other stars and fantastic places. He introduced a new generation to Spin and Marty and Annette Funicello—child stars who became role models for their peer group. Mickey represented possibility and potential, wonder and

9

OPPOSITE: *Mickey conducts the universe in concept art from "The Sorcerer's Apprentice" segment of Fantasia (1940).*

"I have tremendous admiration for him. He represents what it is to be open and innocent. He created mythology that still makes sense to us."

—Henry Geldzahler, former curator of modern paintings at the Metropolitan Museum of Art in New York

imagination. Whenever audiences heard the familiar "Hi, folks!" something great was bound to come next. In the 1950s, it was no longer what Mickey did that mattered, it was what he represented. When Mickey became a character in the parks, the distance that existed between the star and his audience in film and on television was abolished. For the first time, people could walk through the fantasy, and touch it. The imagined became real.

But beyond the shorts, the films, the parks, somewhere along the way Mickey became a citizen of the world. The simple image of Mickey has come to have individual meaning for people of all ages across the globe. One story of Mickey's drawing power was related to Disney artist John Hench by the world-famous "Jungle Doctor," Thomas Dooley, who managed hospital ships in Southeast Asia. He set up stations where he had hoped children would line up for inoculations. Unfortunately, he had trouble getting children and their parents to participate in the program. It wasn't until after he had approached Walt Disney with a request to use Mickey in place of the hospital's Red Cross symbol that children would come anywhere near the lines. With the Mickey flag waving high children couldn't line up fast enough.

Disney's visual language has spread throughout the world. And Mickey Mouse has come to have a life of his own above and beyond his iconic connection with the Walt Disney Company and even America. Sten Jorgensen, who heads up Disney's international magazine group, says, "*Topolino*, first published in 1932, was the first international comic book to feature Mickey Mouse. The popularity of this magazine surged to such a degree . . . that Mickey became solidly anchored in Italian culture. In the eyes of Italian children, he ceases to be American."

Since his birth, nearly three quarters of a century ago, Mickey has become one of the world's most recognizable images. His image is so recognizable and affecting, in fact, that just a glove . . . his shorts . . . the Sorcerer's hat . . . can invoke the delightful imp.

10

"The attraction to Mickey is almost primitive. Kids who scream bloody murder when their parents put them on Santa's lap will run up to Mickey and wrap their arms around his legs."—John Hench, Walt Disney Imagineering

OPPOSITE: The temple of Mickey pyramid display of hand-painted bisque figurines from the collection of Mel Birnkrant

CHAPTER 1

AN
UNLIKELY
HERO

ABOVE: *Mickey puts on his best impersonation of Charles Lindbergh. Animation drawing by Ub Iwerks*

RIGHT: *Walt Disney at his drawing board*

THE BIG BANG

In 1928 when Walt Disney tried to sell Mickey Mouse to film distributors based on the first two cartoons, *Plane Crazy* and *The Gallopin' Gaucho*, he was met with a wave of indifference. "We don't know you," they told him, "and we don't know your mouse." This came as a serious blow to Walt, who had just lost his latest cartoon star, Oswald the Lucky Rabbit—and most of his animation staff—to Universal Pictures. With prospects dimming, Walt and his ace animator Ub Iwerks started on the third Mickey short, but decided to add something that nobody could ignore.

Scene # 2.
Close up of Mickey in cabin of wheel'house, keeping time to last two measures of verse of ' steamboat Bill '. With gesture he starts whistleing the chorus in perfect time to music....his body keeping time with every other beat while his shoulders and foot keep time with each beat. At the end of every two measures he twirls wheel which makes a ratchet sound as it spins. He takes in breath at proper time according to music. When he finishes last measure he reaches up and pulls on whistle cord above his head.
(Use FIFE to imitate his whistle)

LEFT: *Script page containing Iwerks's storysketch of Mickey in the now-classic pose from Steamboat Willie (1928). Disney's notes appear at left and detail the steps used for perfect synchronization of sound and image, a technique now called mickey-mousing.*

OPPOSITE: *Ub Iwerks created the first set of storyboards for Plane Crazy (1928), the first Mickey Mouse cartoon.*

PRECEDING PAGES: *Mickey plays the role of a steam shovel operator in the 1933 short Building a Building.*

15

Al Jolson had become the first voice of film when he cried out—simultaneously singing, speaking, and sobbing—"My Mammy" in blackface in *The Jazz Singer*, which opened at the Warner's Theater in New York in 1927. When Walt saw a screening of the world's first "talkie," he immediately knew he needed to adapt the technology to animation. "I have come to this definite conclusion: sound effects and talking pictures are more than a mere novelty," Walt predicted. "They are here to stay and will develop into a wonderful thing." At great personal expense and with no guarantee of success, Walt, his brother Roy, and animators Iwerks, Wilfred Jackson, Johnny Cannon, and Les Clark created a crude method of synchronizing sound and music with cartoon action.

In 1928, at the tail end of the madcap F. Scott Fitzgerald Jazz Age and one year before the Wall Street stock market crash that led to the Great Depression, a happy-go-lucky, impish, impudent cartoon character named Mickey Mouse made his debut appearance in the first synchronized sound cartoon, *Steamboat Willie*. Following the historic opening on November 18 (a date now regarded as Mickey's official birthday), at the Colony Theatre in New York City, audiences and the world became instantly mad for Mickey, who achieved star status overnight.

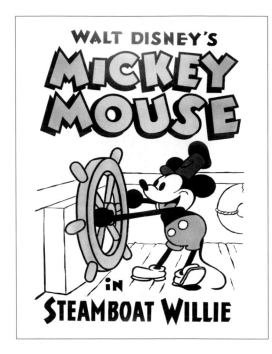

ABOVE: *Poster created for the fiftieth Anniversary of Steamboat Willie*

BELOW LEFT: *Face-to-face with the steamboat captain, Mickey is at once sheepish and defiant.*

BELOW RIGHT: *Animator Ub Iwerks perfects Mickey's design in the months leading up to the mouse's debut.*

16

ABOVE & BELOW RIGHT: *Mickey and Minnie gleefully beat out the rhythm of "Turkey in the Straw."*

When Mickey first "talked," it seemed to audiences to be a miracle that a cartoon character could appear to come to life. *Steamboat Willie* used imaginatively orchestrated music to underscore the squeaks, squeals, screams, and whistles of Mickey and the as yet unnamed Minnie. The score included a pot-and-pan bang-up version of "Turkey in the Straw," which starts as Minnie cranks up a goat's tail after the goat has swallowed her "Turkey" sheet music. Mickey pulls and squeezes a cow's udders, and bangs away at its teeth as if the animal's open mouth were a xylophone. Audiences heard every bang and thump, and they loved it. So did the critics. "It is impossible to describe this riot of mirth," wrote an *Exhibitor's Herald* journalist, "but it knocked me out of my seat." And audiences continued to roar.

17

ABOVE: *Mickey impersonates the Tramp.*

OPPOSITE: Production stills from Plane
Crazy, *Mickey's first and most-
daring adventure, in which he
builds his own plane from materials
at hand and teaches himself how to
fly. Minnie, Mickey's female
twin, plays the concerned copilot.*

Following the success of *Steamboat Willie*, Walt released his
original two Mickey shorts with sound tracks. In *Plane Crazy*,
entirely animated by Iwerks, audiences saw the very first Mickey,
barefoot and gloveless. This film features a tousle-haired Mickey,
looking not unlike another aviator, Charles A. Lindbergh. Adopting
features from earlier cartoon characters like Felix the Cat and his
own Oswald the Lucky Rabbit, Iwerks established the impish
rodent's look.

Silent film star Douglas Fairbanks influenced the swashbuckling
character of Mickey in *The Gallopin' Gaucho*; but it was Charlie Chaplin,
Buster Keaton, and Harold Lloyd who had a more lasting influence
on the comedic antics of the Mouse. Walt himself admitted that in
Mickey there was a deliberate attempt to capture "the wistfulness of
Chaplin—a little fellow trying to do the best he could." The Mouse's
and the Tramp's careers had much in common. In Chaplin's earliest
films for Keystone in 1914, he is often rude, short-tempered, and
even cruel. By 1916, Chaplin had redefined his little Tramp as an
underdog, facing life's challenges with a smile and a jaunty kick-step.
Mickey, too, learned that manners go a long way. As a result, scenes
like the udder-pulling during the "Turkey in the Straw" sequence in
Steamboat Willie would turn up less frequently in the future.

19

Ultimately, however, swashbucklers, pilots, and tramps aside, Walt provided Mickey's voice and true personality. When it came to creating Mickey stories, animator Frank Thomas says, "Only Walt could do it. He was the master Mickey storyteller, and played up Mickey's derring-do."

"Mickey was Walt, and Walt was Mickey."—Animator Frank Thomas

ABOVE: *Mickey Mouse Bubble Gum Company card #21 features Horace Horsecollar, Walt Disney, and Mickey Mouse.*

BELOW: *A self-possessed Mickey struts his stuff in the musical short* The Jazz Fool *(1929).*

Walt, with brother Roy guiding the company's finances, made two dozen films with Mickey from 1928 to 1930, most of which were musicals; *The Barn Dance, The Opry House, Mickey's Follies,* and *The Jazz Fool* played to the public's fascination with "talkies."

20

ABOVE: *Model sheet for the costume drama, Two-Gun Mickey (1934).*

"Mickey Mouse is at one with the Great Common Denominator of the great common art of the commonality in terms of expression ... based on the principle of the triumph of the boob, the cosmic victory of the underdog." —Movie historian Terry Ramsaye, 1932

CAROLINA THEATRE MICKEY MOUSE CLUB

The Home of **MICKEY MOUSE** Cartoons

Sponsored by Charlotte Better Films Committee and Parent-Teachers Assoc.

This Certifies that

No. 1239

MICKEY MOUSE CLUB CREED

I will be a square shooter in my home, in school, on the playground and where ever I may be.

I will be truthful and honorable and strive, always, to make myself a better and more useful little citizen.

I will respect my elders and help the aged, the helpless and children smaller than myself.

In short, I will be a good American!—

ABOVE: *Mickey Mouse Club membership card, complete with Club Creed*

BELOW: *Children discovered the "official" Mickey Mouse Club button among the items in their membership packets.*

OPPOSITE: *Mickey Mouse Club sponsors often provided promotional give-aways to club members, such as the paper mask offered by the Einson- Freeman Company of New York.*

OVERLEAF: *The first Disney song released on sheet music, "Minnie's Yoo Hoo" served as the theme song for the original Mickey Mouse Club.*

22

SQUARE-SHOOTING MICKEY MICE

In September of 1929, theater manager Harry W. Woodin approached Walt with the idea to start the very first Mickey Mouse Club. Walt supported the theater-sponsored clubs wholeheartedly.

The next month, the stock market crashed, and everything changed. Everything, that is, except for Mickey's career—which showed no signs of letting up. Woodin recognized that Mickey remained a thriving success, continuing to draw crowds into theaters despite tough times. It didn't hurt that movie tickets were selling for only 10¢ or 15¢ apiece, offering an inexpensive, quick-fix pleasure. The Disney Studio was producing Mickey shorts at breakneck speeds. Mickey's Golden Age was in full swing.

Saturday, January 11, 1930, at noon, the first official theater-based Mickey Mouse Club opened its doors to kids at the Fox Dome Theater in Ocean Park, California. Woodin invited local merchants and businesses to participate in the program, much to their benefit. Neighborhood bakeries offered up cakes to celebrate the birthdays of Club members each week. Delighted kids would walk away from Club meetings with Mickey Mouse masks, pins, and banners, all sponsored by local or national organizations or the theater managers themselves. Dairies sponsored ice-cream prizes; banks offered piggy banks; and drugstores provided candy and trinkets. And the free goodies won more than the children's hearts—the merchants gained a loyal customer base. And, thus, the Mickey Mouse Clubs became the lifeblood for many merchants during the Depression.

23

MICKEY MOUSE "THEME SONG"
"MINNIE'S YOO HOO"

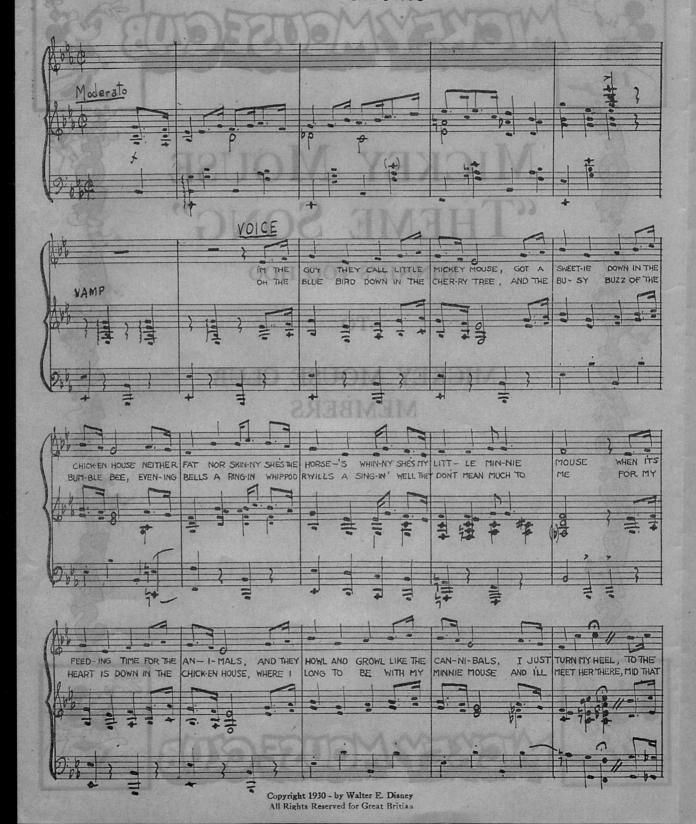

A survey of children in the Depression found that many kids thought Mickey was a dog or cat, even though his last name was Mouse.

ABOVE: *Local theater managers distributed Mickey Mouse Club membership applications to neighborhood children.*

OPPOSITE: *Poster advertising the first meeting of the first Mickey Mouse Club at the Fox Dome Theater in Ocean Park, California*

Within the first year, hundreds of these early Mickey Mouse Clubs were formed across America, Canada, and in Great Britain. Parents happily sent their "Mickey Mice" into the theaters where they participated in wholesome activities that promoted good citizenship.

By 1932, the Clubs boasted more than a million members in the United States alone, approximating the combined memberships of the Boy Scouts and Girl Scouts of America. Within four years of the first British Mickey Mouse Club, more than four hundred new branches popped up across the Atlantic (presumably omitting the "good American" from their Club Creed).

SEE PIG DANCE
FROM SHINDIG

USE SAME PAN
AS (40)

28

A MOUSE FOR ALL MERCHANTS

Success could not be confined merely to motion pictures and a children's fan club. The first Mickey Mouse collectible, a writing tablet, appeared in 1930 and led to a steady stream of products. But it wasn't until 1932, when Walt hired advertising maestro Herman "Kay" Kamen to head up the studio's fledgling merchandising department, that the Mickey Mouse merchandising explosion began. Working from his New York office, Kamen signed over licenses to scores of companies clamoring to use Mickey's name and image on their merchandise.

ABOVE: *Merchandising guru Kay Kamen's stationery letterhead, circa 1932*

RIGHT: *$300 cash bought the rights to use Mickey's image on the first piece of Mickey Mouse merchandise, a grammar school writing tablet created in 1930.*

OPPOSITE: *Mickey's lighthearted attitude gets the joint jumping. Storyboard drawings from The Whoopee Party (1932).*

29

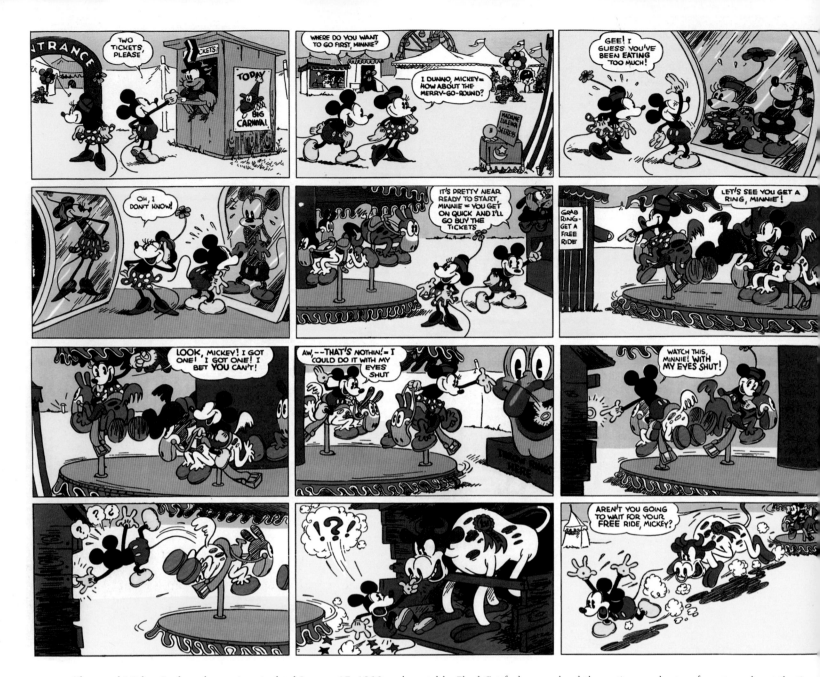

In 1930, Mickey was seen in a comic strip for King Features, the first Mickey book was published by Bibo-Lang, and Mickey Mouse toys were flooding the United States and European markets. At Woolworth's toy department, a dime could buy a Mickey Mouse Big Little Book, a wind-up toy, or a bisque Mickey Mouse figurine. Dime stores across the country sold countless Mickey Mouse items in ten-cent bins: tin-litho wind-ups, celluloids, moving or walking wooden Mickey pull toys, coloring books, china sets, painted

LEFT: *The Mickey Mouse Target game, produced by the Marks Brothers Corporation, included a cardboard target, a pellet gun, and rubber bullets.*

BELOW. *Mickey and Minnie Mouse decorate a children's china tea set.*

BELOW: *Wooden alphabet blocks featuring Mickey and his Barnyard Pals*

BELOW RIGHT: *Mickey Mouse magazine advertisement for a Mickey Mouse flashlight and batteries*

bisque toothbrush holders, puzzles, framed Mickey pictures, boxed board-game sets, target boards with darts, alphabet-block sets, paint and printing sets, plug-in toy stoves with electrical heating units, balloons, domino sets, toothbrushes, combs, and fountain pens. During the most troubled economic period America experienced in the last century, the public's thirst for Mickey persisted.

31

32   The Mickey Mouse handcar reportedly saved the Lionel Train Company from bankruptcy in 1934. The number 1100 Mickey Mouse handcar featured Mickey and Minnie with arms pumping up and down in a seesaw manner. The action toy came in a colorful box, complete with eight sections of a curved metal track to form a 27" circle. The metal 7½" wind-up with painted wood-composition Mickey and Minnie figures sold for a dollar in 1934 and quickly became a "must-have" to circle around the Christmas tree that year. Subsequently, in 1935 the Lionel Train Corporation put into the marketplace a Mickey Mouse Circus Train set featuring a heavy metal red Commander Vanderbilt engine car, a coal-shoveling Mickey Mouse stoker, and three metal cars with brightly colored lithographic decorations—a band car, a circus car, and a dining car—all incorporating Mickey and other Disney characters into the design. The set included a freestanding painted wood composition Mickey Mouse circus-barker figurine and a cardboard Lionel Mickey Mouse circus tent—all for two dollars.

RIGHT: *The Depression Era short Mickey's Follies (1929) has Mickey and his friends making do with the materials within reach during a jam session. This short featured Mickey's theme song, "Minnie's Yoo Hoo."*

BELOW: *The Ingersoll-Waterbury Clock Company produced the first Mickey Mouse wristwatch in 1933.*

"Mickey Mouse Emerges as Economist: Citizen of the World, Unexplained Phenomenon, He Wins Victories in the Field of Businessman and Banker"—L. H. Robbins, *The New York Times* headline, March 10, 1935

The year 1933, regarded by many historians as the worst of the Depression, saw the first Mickey Mouse watch, produced by Ingersoll-Waterbury Clock Company. That year alone, Mickey received 800,000 fan letters—more than any other Hollywood star. Sales of the Ingersoll watch skyrocketed, and the time-telling Mickey managed to take that company out of receivership. The watch became such an icon that it—along with other items that reflected American culture—was put into a time capsule in a special ceremony at the 1939–1940 World's Fair in Queens, New York, and lowered deep into the ground.

33

Mickey contemplates commitment and parenthood in Mickey's Nightmare (1932). Mickey's peaceful dream of life married to Minnie takes a turbulent turn with the arrival of baby mice. Mickey wakes to his loyal pal Pluto, licking his face, relieved to find that it is still a bachelor's life for him.

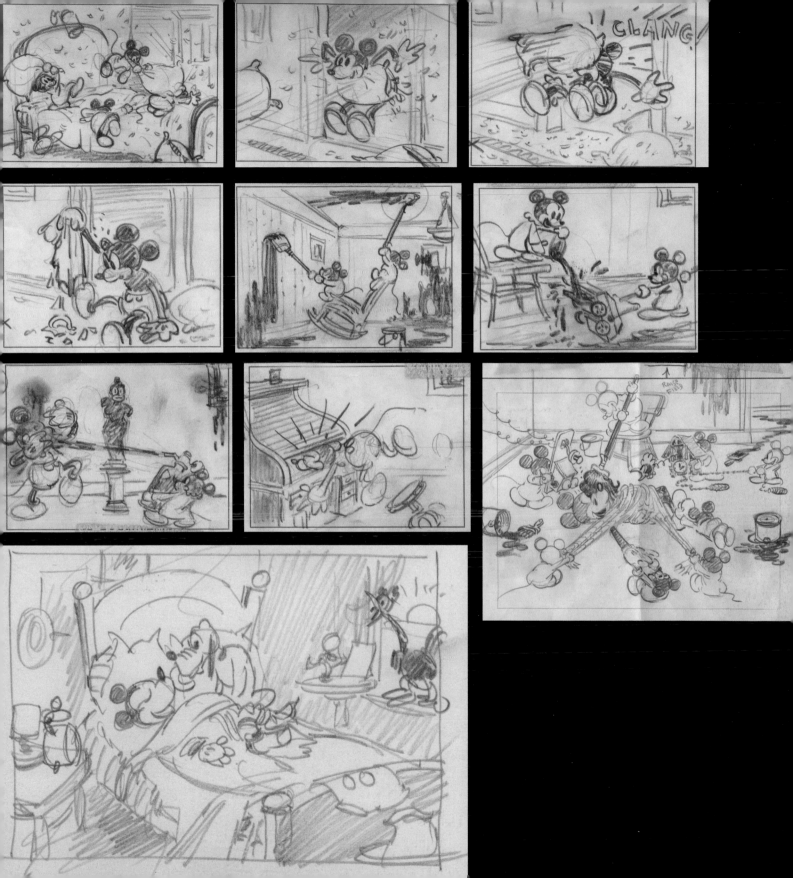

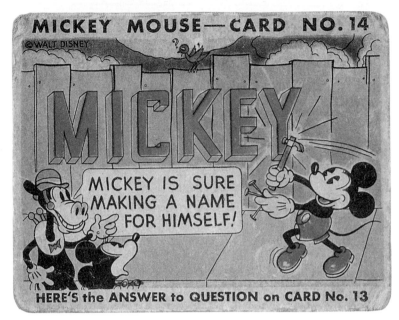

ABOVE: Mickey Mouse Bubble Gum
Company collector card #14

LEFT: Mickey's star power was confirmed on
November 3, 1978, when he was added to
Hollywood's Walk of Fame between Sir Elton
John and Jack Nicholson.

RIGHT: Model sheet pose from
Touchdown Mickey (1932)

"Poor Mickey is in the hands of the dilettantes. After escaping
hundreds of other dreadful perils, he is now in the most
desperate plight of his career." —*Women's Home Companion*, 1934

OPPOSITE: Poster for The Klondike
Kid (1932), Mickey's forty-ninth
short, in which he saves Minnie
from the elements, and from the
dastardly villain Peg Leg Pierre

OVERLEAF: Centerfold pullout poster
featuring Mickey Mouse
as it appeared in the
Motion Picture Herald

36

TOAST OF THE TOWN

In Hollywood, Mickey Mouse received acclaim right alongside Greta Garbo and Walt's own favorite comic actor— Charlie Chaplin. With the release of the cartoon *Just Mickey* in 1930, the Mouse landed his own entry in Hollywood's Directory of Actors, thus: Height: 2' 3"; Weight: 23 lbs.; Agent: Walt Disney. In 1932, Walt Disney won a special Academy Award for the creation of Mickey Mouse. Mickey appeared in *Who's Who in America* and the 1934 new edition of the *Encyclopædia Britannica*.

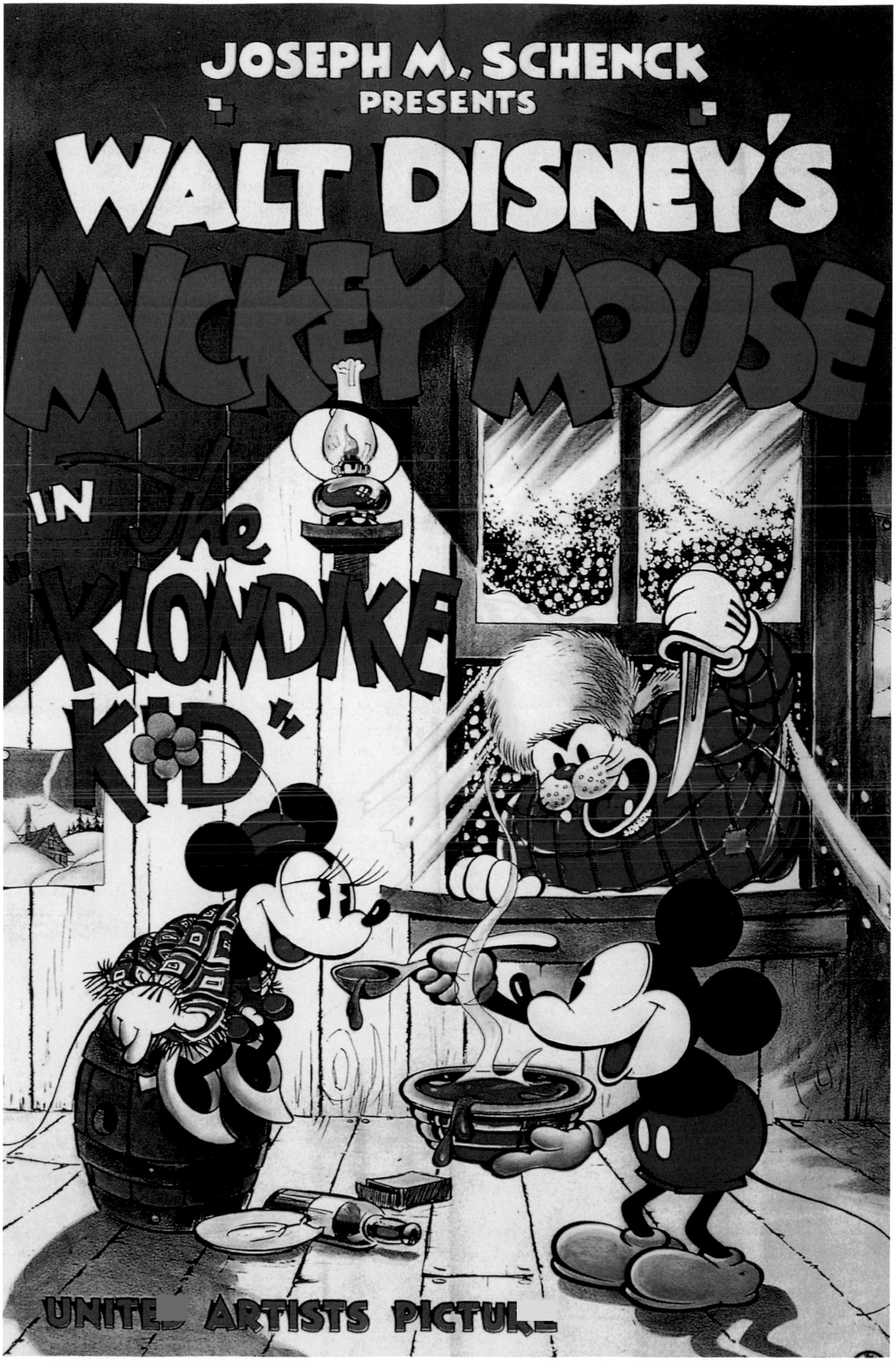

THE SCREEN'S MOST P

MICKEY

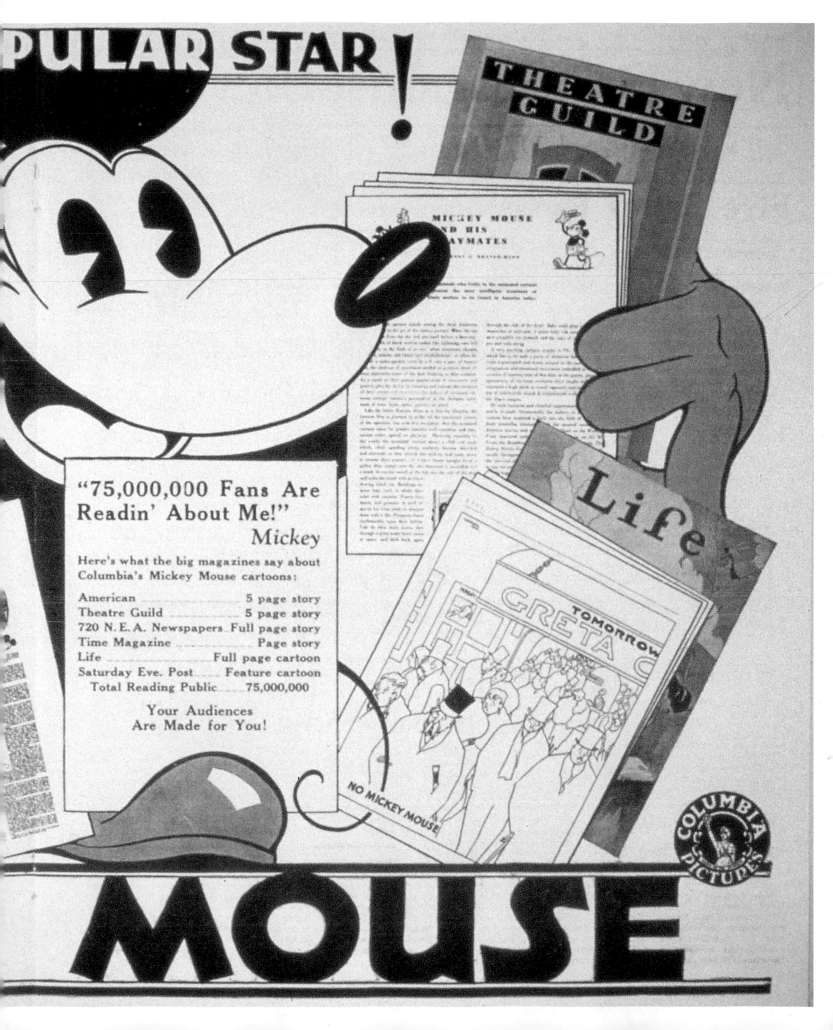

PULAR STAR!

THEATRE GUILD

"75,000,000 Fans Are Readin' About Me!" Mickey

Here's what the big magazines say about Columbia's Mickey Mouse cartoons:

American	5 page story
Theatre Guild	5 page story
720 N.E.A. Newspapers	Full page story
Time Magazine	Page story
Life	Full page cartoon
Saturday Eve. Post	Feature cartoon
Total Reading Public	75,000,000

Your Audiences Are Made for You!

Life

MOUSE

COLUMBIA PICTURES

"Mickey lives in a world in which space, time, and the laws of physics are nil. He can reach inside of a bull's mouth, pull out his teeth and use them for castanets. He can lead a band or play violin solos; his ingenuity is limitless; he never fails." —*Time Magazine*, February 16, 1931

ABOVE: *Mickey toasts the stars of Hollywood in this promotional poster for Mickey's Gala Premiere (1933).*

ABOVE RIGHT: *Detail from a 3-sheet movie poster created for MGM's Hollywood Party featuring Laurel and Hardy and Lupe Velez*

OPPOSITE: *Model sheet from The Band Concert (1935), the first color Mickey Mouse cartoon*

Mickey's star status also led to appearances in live-action feature films produced by film studios other than Disney, including the 1934 *Hollywood Party*, an all-star comedy with guest appearances by Laurel and Hardy, Lupe Velez, Jimmy Durante, Polly Moran, the Ziegfeld stage star Marilyn Miller, Charles Butterworth, and Ted Healy and the Stooges. Hal Roach, the original producer of the *Our Gang* comedy series cast an unusual incarnation of a roguish Mickey in a three-dimensional doll-like form in his Laurel and Hardy extravaganza, *Babes in Toyland* (1934). This weird Mickey and his companion, the Cat and the Fiddle, ponder what to do about Tom-Tom the Piper's son who has been falsely accused of pig stealing. At a later point in this black-and-white classic, Mickey boards a miniature blimp and bombs a marching toy army of roustabout troublemakers with firecrackers before bailing out and parachuting to safety himself.

The world of food products was eager to embrace Mickey in the 1930s and has been ever since. A perfect salesman, Mickey's image could be found on milk, bread, Post Toasties Cereal, Mickey Mouse Soda Pop, Mickey Mouse Chocolate bars, Mickey Mouse Jujubes (sticky candy molded into the shape of Mickey), Mickey Mouse Chewing Gum, Mickey Mouse Bubble Gum, Mickey Mouse Butter Creams, Mickey Mouse Comic Cookies and Wafers, and Mickey Mouse Jam (Marmalade, in Britain).

42

Mickey developed a following of fans among notables, including Franklin and Eleanor Roosevelt, who regularly showed Mickey cartoons at the White House; Mary Pickford, who said publicly that Mickey Mouse was her very favorite star; and child stars Shirley Temple and Jane Withers, both of whom had collected many Mickey dolls. Marion Davies once had a Mickey Mouse party at Hearst castle in San Simeon, California, where all the guests came dressed as Disney characters and other cartoon stars of the day.

"He is not a little mouse," Walt said of his creation. "He only looks like one. He is Youth, the Great Unlicked and Uncontaminated."

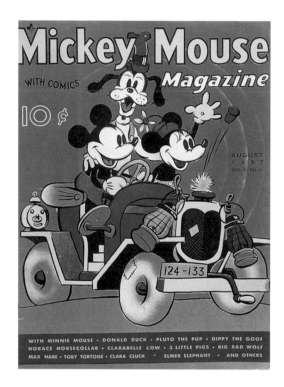

ABOVE LEFT: *Child star Shirley Temple serves tea to Dickie Moore in 1936 in the company of her Mickey and Minnie Mouse dolls.*

ABOVE: *Mickey Mouse Magazine cover*

OPPOSITE: *Production stills from Mickey's Birthday Party (1931)*

44

ODDBALL MICKEYS

Mickey Mouse Milk of Magnesia toothpaste got boys and girls to brush their teeth with their very own Mickey Mouse toothbrush, which was always waiting inside the arm of the bisque Mickey Mouse toothbrush holder.

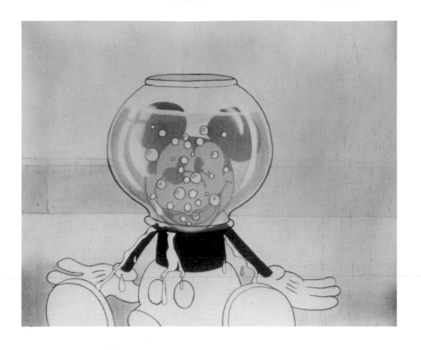

"Perhaps Mickey's celebrity is not so amazing, after all, when one remembers that he came to us at the time the country needed him most—at the beginning of the Depression. He has helped us laugh away our troubles, forget our creditors and keep our chins up."

—Edwin C. Hill, *Boston American*, August 8, 1933

45

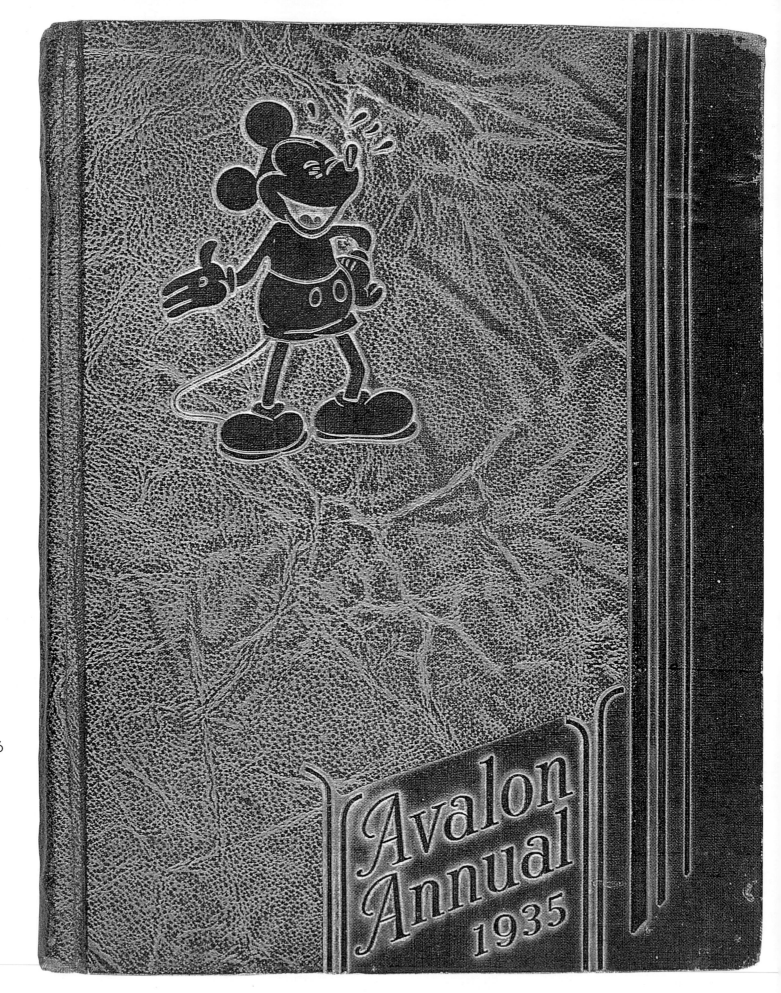

Avalon
Annual
1935

MICKEY GIVES AN

ADDRESS

MICKEY IN

SCHOOL

"Mickey was the first cartoon character to stress personality. I thought of him from the first as a distinct individual, not just a cartoon type of symbol going through comedy routines."—Walt Disney

The Student Body of Avalon, Pennsylvania High School wrote to and received permission from Walt Disney himself to illustrate their 1935 yearbook with Mickey Mouse drawings.

"Energetic without being elevated...he is never sentimental, indeed, there is a scandalous element in him which I find most restful."—E. M. Forster

THIS PAGE: *Post Toasties cardboard cut-outs show daredevil Mickey as he takes a spin and a fall on his roller skates.*

ROLE-MODEL MICKEY

Mickey became a bona fide icon to the masses in the Depression decade simply by making people laugh; but Mickey's success would come to haunt him. As the merchandise continued to sell and his popularity grew to monumental status, he became such an influence on children (and their parents) that before long he was not allowed to do the very things that made him a star in the first place. Angry mothers sent letters to Walt Disney, claiming that their children imitated Mickey's merry mischief-making pranks; and that he ought to become a better example and role model in terms of good behavior. "Mickey was on a pedestal," Walt recalled years later. The Mouse was by now so heavily monitored that the only choice was to hand over the action and comedy to his volatile supporting players: Goofy, Pluto, and especially Donald Duck. Unlike Mickey, "the duck could blow his top," Walt noted. "Then I tied Pluto and Donald together. The stupid things Pluto would do, along with the duck, gave us an outlet for our gags." After 1936 shorts *Mickey's Rival* and *Thru the Mirror*, Mickey would never carry a film again, acting instead as straight man or master of ceremonies in his own cartoons, and ceding most of the action and comedy to his former sidekicks, many of whom, in addition to supporting Mickey, had their own series by 1938.

48

OPPOSITE & OVERLEAF: *Mickey dreams that he steps through his mirror to find animated objects on the other side in* Thru the Mirror (1936), *production stills (opposite) and story-board drawings (overleaf). A nod to Lewis Carroll's* Through the Looking Glass, *the short features Mickey dancing and playing with a deck of cards. He revels in the fun until the jealous King of Hearts chases Astaire Mickey back to the other side of the mirror.*

"CARDS: SHUFFLE!"

"CARDS CUT!"

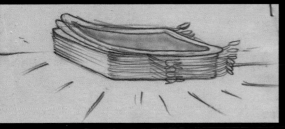

CARDS GOOSE MICKEY

Regardless of angry moms, Mickey Mouse cartoons achieved phenomenal success at the movies, and attendance fell off greatly at theaters that did not advertise Disney shorts. The title of a song written by Irving Caesar, "What, No Mickey Mouse?" became a phrase used by moviegoers in the 1930s when a theater did not include a Mickey cartoon along with their feature presentations.

"MICKEY MOUSE ALSO JOAN CRAWFORD AND CLARK GABLE"

—Kansas City theater marquee, 1935

ABOVE: *Pantages theater marquee in Hollywood highlights Tallulah Bankhead in Tarnished Lady and a Mickey Mouse comedy.*

OPPOSITE: *Sheet music cover for the Irving Caesar song "What! No Mickey Mouse?" published in 1932*

McCALL'S MICKEY

Walt Disney and his brother Roy were enchanted by the stuffed Mickey Mouse dolls created by Charlotte Clark in 1930. The 12" to 20" dolls, designed from sketches made by Clark's fourteen-year-old nephew, Bob Clampett, usually sold for five dollars at better department stores like Bullock's in Los Angeles. The five-dollar price tag was not affordable to most American families whose breadwinner considered himself lucky to make a salary of ten dollars a week.

One solution was to offer Clark's Mickey dolls through the McCall Company of New York, originally developed as an offshoot of *McCall's Magazine*. The first McCall Printed Mickey Mouse Pattern #91 was made available to the market in 1932 at a cost of 35¢; and these became a hit with homemakers and seamstresses in America, Canada, Spain, and Great Britain from 1932 to 1939. Mickey or Minnie Mouse dolls could be made at home with 8 1/2", 13 1/2", and 18" cut-out doll patterns purchased at sewing centers, dime stores, department stores, or through *McCall's Magazine* by mail order.

52

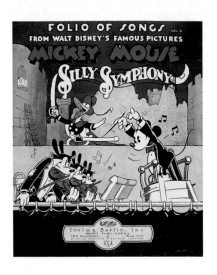

"**You're a melody from a symphony by Strauss/ You're a Bendel bonnet/A Shakespeare sonnet/ You're Mickey Mouse!**"—Cole Porter, lyric from "You're the Top"

OPPOSITE: *The first performance of Ireland's Mickey Mouse Orchestra at the Theatre Royal in Dublin*

MICKEY MOUSE MUSIC

"Mickey Mouse music" is a Jazz Age style based on hotel dance orchestras of the twenties and thirties, as well as the top recording bands such as those led by Paul Whiteman, George Olson, and Anson Weeks, or Rudy Vallee and his Connecticut Yankees. The more serious film composers who created full orchestrated scores for dramatic movies coined the term "Mickey Mouse music" to describe the ricky-tick–saxophonia–percussion-faster-than-fast syncopated beat, much of which had emerged out of the Dixieland style of the 1920s that emanated from New Orleans, Chicago, and Harlem.

Some of the early films with distinct musical themes include: *The Barn Dance*, *The Barnyard Broadcast*, *The Jazz Fool*, *Jungle Rhythm*, and *Mickey's Revue*. In *Whoopee Party*, Minnie, at the piano, plays "Sweet Rosie O'Grady" and Mickey belts out "Maple Leaf Rag." Other barnyard guests join in dancing on a frantic upbeat version of "Runnin' Wild." At one point the entire house moves, almost exploding to the sound of the music. Everything grooves to the music, including snapping mousetraps, chairs, tables, lamps, and coffeepots. The ironing board starts to sway while the shirts on the line create their own dance to the rhythm of the music.

Sheet music and song folios usually found on the living room upright piano in the 1920s and 1930s were often purchased at a dime store or at a music store where a glamorous piano-playing vocalist with electro-permanent-wave "Blondex"-hair, jungle-red "Tangee" lips, and heavily mascaraed eyes might be found. She'd probably be crooning in the manner of a Busby Berkeley dame such hit Mickey Mouse songs as "Mickey and Minnie's in Town," "The Wedding of Mr. Mickey Mouse," or "Mickey Mouse's Birthday Party."

54

56

Mickey's intelligence enabled him to be resourceful and ingenious when facing a bully. Ultimately, Mickey's heart and soul were Walt Disney's. "I always felt Walt's presence very strongly when I worked with Mickey," animator Ollie Johnston recalls. "Mickey did a lot of the things Walt had wanted to do—rescuing princesses, standing up to bullies, putting on variety shows." Usually smaller than his adversaries, Mickey had to rely on his brains rather than brawn.

By decade's end, one thing was clear—audiences loved watching little Mickey triumph against the odds. "I guess the cartoon is something everyone knows and likes," Walt remarked early on, at a loss to explain the phenomenon he had unleashed.

"Mickey is 'Everyman,' battling for life and love against a devil who is both villain and chief comedian of the piece. Mickey had his little weaknesses but there is no question which side he is on. He is like David who slays Goliath. The little man who shuts his eyes and pastes the big bully in the jaw."—Arthur Millier, *Los Angeles Times*, November 5, 1933

CHAPTER 2

CITIZEN
MICKEY

MAN OR MOUSE?

Mickey developed more than a following in the first ten years of his career: he developed character. Gone were the days when Mickey's presence on the screen amounted to nothing more than impulsive pranks and Keystone comedy antics. He relinquished his slapstick, gag-driven roles to his barnyard pals.

Exhibiting his maturity, Mickey sought out select straight-man roles, passing numerous opportunities on to his costars. In the 1940s, Mickey appeared in only eleven shorts—a far cry from the previous decade's eighty-seven. Pluto and Goofy cut loose as top dogs, starring in thirty-six and twenty-three of their own shorts, respectively. Donald eclipsed all three careers combined by racking up seventy-two shorts in ten years. Not the jealous type, Mickey graciously shared the limelight. "His attitude is that of the older master who's glad to give the youngsters a hand," Walt told *New York Times* film critic Frank Nugent in 1947 about Mickey's place at the studio. "The Mouse knows we have to keep bringing new people along, new faces. It makes his job that much easier. It was pretty tough when he was carrying the whole studio. But now he's got the Duck and Pluto and the Goof."

60

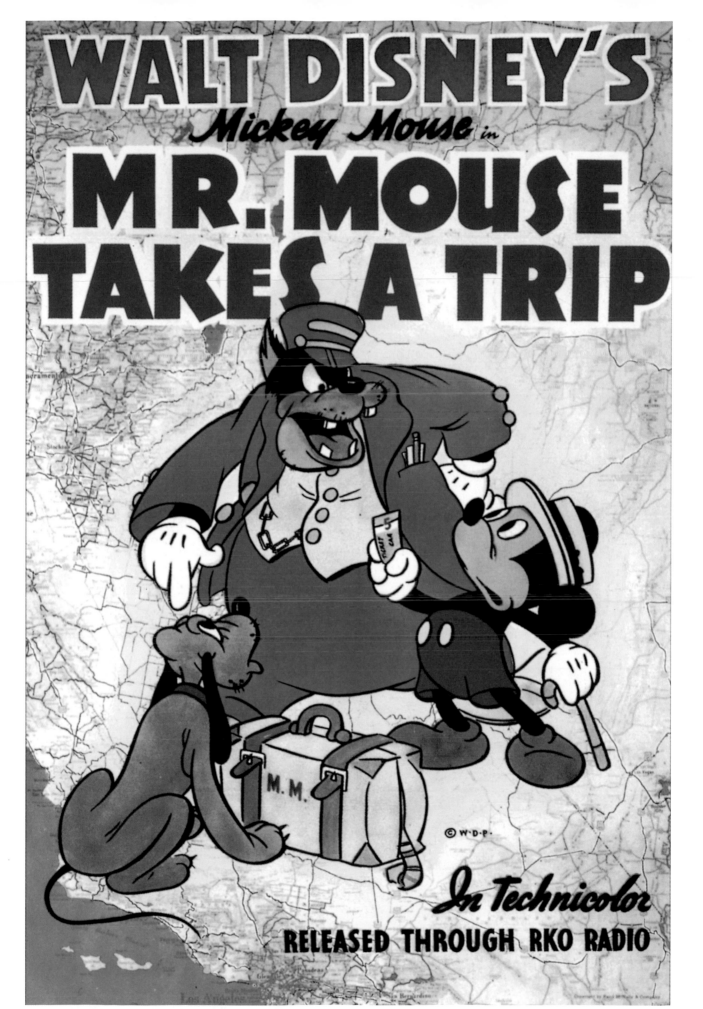

Model sheet and production stills from the Academy Award *nominated short* The Pointer *(1939). The short evidenced the first use of animator Fred Moore's softer, humanoid design for Mickey. The most notable change Moore made was to the eyes—once black ovals, Mickey's eyes now contained whites and pupils to increase his expressiveness.*

In response to the casting of Mickey in "good citizen" roles, animators softened his look and made him cuter. His redesign first appeared in *The Pointer* (1939). Mickey no longer donned his classic red shorts and yellow shoes; instead, he sported contemporary garb. His round body became more pear-shaped, the slope of his forehead gave way to a more rounded noggin, and his face developed a hint of color as well as pinchable cheeks. Mickey's makeover included another, albeit short-lived change. He lost an expressive appendage: his tail. Animators calculated thousands of hours and dollars could be saved simply by eliminating that single

- NOTE -
Adult quail are same
as used in "Snow White"
Baby quail are
slightly different
as portrayed
below.

Keep bear bulky
and powerful looking,
also the jaws should
be carried big.

The POINTER
RM-27 ©
Walt Disney
Prod.

Use wings on
baby quail only
when action
may call for
it.

MICKEY'S HUNTING OUTFIT -

COMPARATIVE SIZE OF BEAR AND MICKEY

63

black line. So for a time, beginning in the late 1930s, as in *Brave Little Tailor* (1938), Mickey appeared *sans queue*. But Mickey's tail proved to be as important as the nose on his face, and it was put back into action. Perhaps the most significant change of the period was to his eyes. Mickey started life with small black pupils inside large white goggle-eyes. By the third film, "a strange condition arose," note animators Frank Thomas and Ollie Johnston in *The Illusion of Life*. The whites of his eyes were so big, viewers mistook

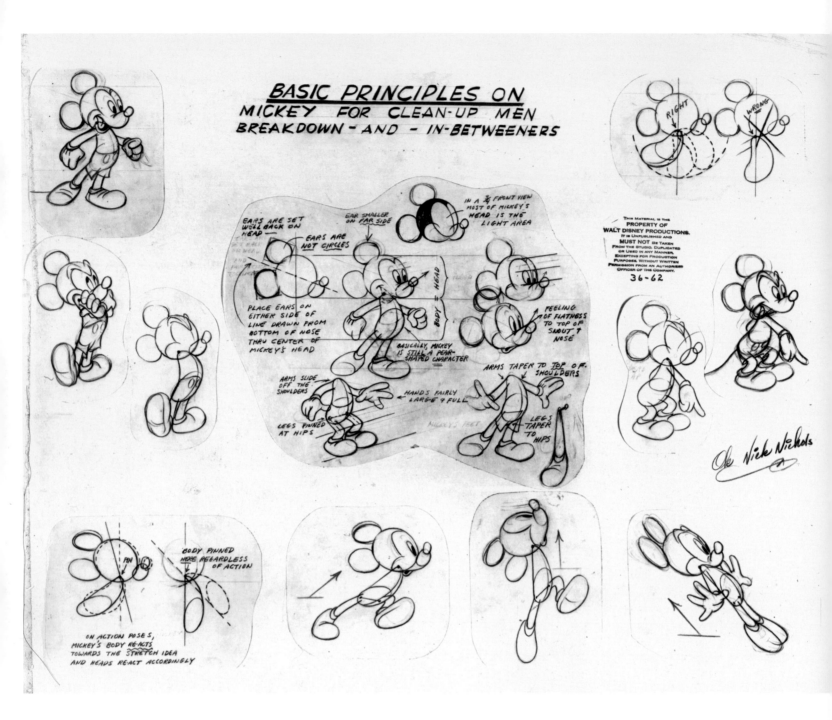

BASIC PRINCIPLES ON
MICKEY FOR CLEAN-UP MEN
BREAKDOWN - AND - IN-BETWEENERS

RIGHT   WRONG

EARS ARE SET WELL BACK ON HEAD

EARS ARE NOT CIRCLES

EAR SMALLER ON FAR SIDE

IN A ¾ FRONT VIEW MOST OF MICKEY'S HEAD IS THE LIGHT AREA

PLACE EARS ON EITHER SIDE OF LINE DRAWN FROM BOTTOM OF NOSE THRU CENTER OF MICKEY'S HEAD

BODY ≠ HEAD

HEAD

BASICALLY, MICKEY IS STILL A PEAR-SHAPED CHARACTER

FEELING OF FLATNESS TO TOP OF SNOUT & NOSE

ARMS TAPER TO TOP OF SHOULDERS

ARMS SLIDE OFF THE SHOULDERS

HAND'S FAIRLY LARGE & FULL

LEGS PINNED AT HIPS

MICKEY'S FEET

LEGS TAPER TO HIPS

THIS MATERIAL IS THE PROPERTY OF WALT DISNEY PRODUCTIONS. IT IS UNPUBLISHED AND MUST NOT BE TAKEN FROM THE STUDIO, DUPLICATED OR USED IN ANY MANNER, EXCEPTING FOR PRODUCTION PURPOSES, WITHOUT WRITTEN PERMISSION FROM AN AUTHORIZED OFFICER OF THE COMPANY.

36-62

De Nick Nichols

PIN

BODY PINNED HERE REGARDLESS OF ACTION

ON ACTION POSES, MICKEY'S BODY RE-ACTS TOWARDS THE STRETCH IDEA AND HEADS RE-ACT ACCORDINGLY

---

64   ABOVE & OPPOSITE: Model sheets document the evolution of Mickey's design. In addition to the change in Mickey's eyes, Moore made Mickey rounder, and instructed other animators on how to make the mouse's body "squash and stretch."

them for his forehead. As Johnston and Thomas remark, "the pupils were now considered to be the whole eye, a solid, black eye like that on a doll." As a result, when Mickey moved his pupils from side to side, or in frustration (as seen in *The Band Concert*), his eyes appeared to roam across his forehead. In the new design, attributed to artist Fred Moore, Mickey suddenly had pupils inside his pupils! Animators now found Mickey much easier to draw, but for many fans this shift to a more "human eye" changed him irrevocably. Author John Updike referred to it as "an evolutionary mistake," noting that the change "took away something of his vitality, his alertness, his bug-eyed cartoon readiness for adventure."

ABOVE: *Production still from* The Band Concert (1935)

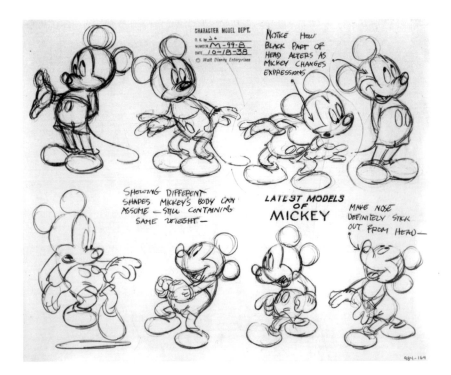

EVERYMAN MICKEY

Hollywood genius director Preston Sturges paid a special tribute to Mickey Mouse in his 1941 classic Paramount film Sullivan's Travels. When overworked chain-gang prisoners watch a Mickey Mouse cartoon and burst into raucous laughter at Mickey's antics, fellow prisoner John Sullivan recognizes that laughter is one of the most important means of escape. Inspired and reawakened by the one and only Mickey Mouse, Sullivan manages to break out of jail and vows to make better and better Hollywood screwball comedies.

6

"What is Mickey anyway, but an abstract idea always in the process of becoming?" —Disney scholar Robert D. Feild

ABOVE LEFT: *Animation of the eager apprentice*

ABOVE RIGHT: *The Sorcerer's conjuring makes a grand impression on his apprentice. Storyboard art*

OPPOSITE & OVERLEAF: *Mickey allows his curiosity to get the best of him. Concept art*

THE SORCERER'S APPRENTICE

Even though Mickey's appearance in shorts was on the wane, Walt had big plans for his little mouse. While deep in production on *Snow White and the Seven Dwarfs*, Walt came up with a plan to revitalize Mickey's career: Mickey would star in a cartoon version of Dukas's classic musical work "The Sorcerer's Apprentice." Although others in the studio were jockeying for *Snow White's* Dopey to land the role, Walt stood firm on his decision to cast Mickey in the non-speaking part. This project launched Mickey into a new level of stardom. When the Mouse with the power of the universe at his fingertips is humbled by his own shortcomings, his audience connects to him on a core level, reveling in his spirit as well as his humanity.

By the time "Sorcerer" was finished, Walt had engaged the imposing Leopold Stokowski to conduct, and the budget for the short cartoon had ballooned to $125,000—making it impossible to break even. The only hope for possible recuperation would be to build a feature around the short; thus the genesis of *Fantasia*. As with *Steamboat Willie*, Walt resolved to think big: he eventually created the first motion picture with a stereo sound track, despite the fact that the vast majority of theatres lacked the proper equipment or technology to present the film. Mickey celebrated this feat by personally congratulating his conductor.

On November 13, 1940, *Fantasia* premiered at the Broadway Theater in New York, formerly the Colony Theater where *Steamboat Willie* had premiered almost twelve years before, to the date. Critics lauded "The Sorcerer's Apprentice" as Mickey's greatest performance. But *Fantasia*, as a whole, opened to mixed reviews and lukewarm business, offering no immediate dividends to Mickey or Walt. Only decades later would the film achieve the status of classic.

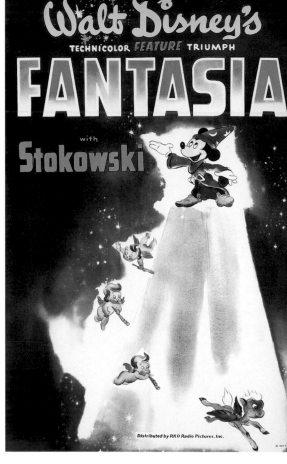

70

ABOVE: *Mickey's prominence on the poster for the original 1940 release of Fantasia underscores the import Walt Disney assigned to "The Sorcerer's Apprentice" segment of his concert feature.*

LEFT: *Animation of Fred Moore's redesigned mouse*

ABOVE: *Concept art of Mickey conducting the universe*

Thoughts of *Fantasia*, Mickey Mouse, and virtually everything else became secondary when Japan attacked the United States naval base at Pearl Harbor on December 7, 1941. The very next day, the United States government commandeered Walt Disney Studios for the purpose of producing military training and propaganda films. With little choice, Walt threw himself and his resources wholeheartedly into the war effort.

"Mr. Stokowski ... Mr. Stokowski ... My congratulations, sir."—Mickey

"Congratulations to you, Mickey!"—Leopold Stokowski

GOODWILL TOUR

On the eve of World War II, President Franklin D. Roosevelt recognized that Mickey Mouse was a beloved figure in South America. Because of Mickey's exalted status, FDR knew that Walt Disney would be an ideal candidate to further the United States' Good Neighbor Policy. The president, who aimed to strengthen relations with South American countries, approached Disney to lead a Goodwill Tour in the spring of 1941. Walt agreed, and that summer traveled with a select team of animators and artists from the studio. Upon their return, the group drew upon the cultural experience of the tour to create *Saludos Amigos* (1943) and *The Three Caballeros* (1945), starring Donald Duck and new pals José Carioca and Panchito. But during their travels, the real star was Mickey Mouse. Everywhere the group went, they were greeted by children anxious to meet the Mouse's creators. Even those who spoke no English knew Mickey Mouse and eagerly asked for his portrait.

ON THE HOME FRONT

During the years of World War II, Mickey as a role model came to symbolize America in the same way Uncle Sam did, and in that regard, it was only natural that he joined the top ranks of those Disney characters who helped to sell war bonds and build ships, tanks, and planes in the "Back the Attack" effort to win the war. Mickey often appeared emblazoned on military insignia, on U. S. government and Allied war posters, and as nose-art on aircraft. Of the more than twelve hundred pieces of Disney Studio military art used for squadron and training corps insignia for the Army, Navy, Air Force, Marines, Coast Guard, and other branches of the service, Mickey placed fourth, behind Donald (with an astonishing 216 different appearances), Pluto, and Goofy. The Three Little Pigs joined the Big Bad Wolf, centaurettes, alligators, and other characters from *Fantasia*; the Seven Dwarfs; Jose Carioca—the South American parrot; Mexico's gun-totin' rooster Panchito; Pablo Penguin; Elmer Elephant; and other Silly Symphony characters.

Mickey's role-model status kept his appearances on World War II *insignia tame as compared with other Disney characters like Peg Leg Pete (below), who often brandished weapons.*

OVERLEAF: *V for Victory! The cover of an ink blotter produced by the Sunoco Oil Company encouraged Americans to buy Sunoco Oil and defense bonds to support the war effort.*

73

DEFEND

© WALT DISNEY PRODUCTIONS

FORM A-920   600M   3-42

Keep 'Em Flying!

BUY DEFENSE BONDS

YOUR CAR'S LIFE
SUNOCO
OIL
Reinforced – to make
otors run better longer!

YOU DIRTY RAT!

During the war years, Mickey not only lent his image to the volunteer branches of the Allied Forces, but appeared on bombs and, unofficially, on German Luftwaffe aircraft. Children from both sides of the Maginot Line looked to Mickey as a talisman that helped them through those scary times. Artist Tomi Ungerer, an Alsatian who lived under Nazi rule during the German occupation of his homeland, found that drawing Mickey Mouse in military gear made him feel safe. His Uncle Heino destroyed his drawings, believing, as Hitler did, that Disney and Mickey Mouse were degenerate tools of capitalism. Few drawings survived his uncle's raids.

While the Duck could rage and fume at the enemy, Mickey, a more gentle guy, kept the home fires burning and the factories churning out war machinery to help the Allied Forces in their fight for freedom. At least thirty-five home-front insignia designs by the Disney Studios employed Mickey as a mascot for the Red Cross, the Junior Victory Army of America, and others, including his roles as an air raid warden and as a volunteer who called upon civilians to Go to Work!

In the end, at least eighty-five percent of the studio's entire output during this period was war-related. Goofy, Donald, and Pluto continued their respective cartoon series, with the latter two joining the armed forces. These adventures fit their feisty personalities perfectly. Even Minnie Mouse had stepped forward, starring in a public service film, *Out of the Frying Pan into the Firing Line* (1942), and in her first short without her beau, *First Aiders* (1944).

"Mickey Mouse is an international hero, better known than Roosevelt or Hitler, a part of the folklore of the world."

—*Fortune Magazine*, November, 1934

LEFT: *Mickey marches to war on a three-dimensional cardboard plaque, produced by the Youngstown Pressed Steel Co. in 1942.*

OVERLEAF: *World War II posters present Mickey eagerly supporting homefront initiatives.*

ABOVE: *Donald Duck led the pack of Disney characters in the number of appearances in Allied posters and insignias. Unlike Mickey, the petulant Duck was allowed to take his place on the frontlines.*

BELOW: *WWII Mickey Mouse Gas Masks encouraged youngsters to wear the contraptions during air raids. The masks were packaged in a playful box that featured Mickey himself donning the ominous apparatus.*

By and large, Mickey was seen on the home turf, representing aircraft workers or Air Force hospital bases; however, the Mouse still managed to make his way to the front: in the bartering of watches that went on between Russian and American soldiers, Mickey Mouse watches fetched very high prices, selling for a thousand dollars each. A more ominous role for Mickey was the "Mickey Mouse Gas Mask" designed by the Sun Rubber Company of Ohio. Although gas attacks never posed a real threat in the United States, Mickey helped alleviate the fear of war for children in Great Britain. Pretending these were for playtime activities, the Mickey Mouse "Small Child Respirator" required that British kids wear them during air raids.

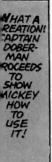

By 1942, Mickey had all but disappeared from the silver screen, appearing in only two films that year, and none at all in 1943, 1944, or 1945. Mickey fared much better in his long-running comic strip, where, thanks to artist Floyd Gottfredson, he retained his early, brash personality in an endless parade of delightful adventures, battling shysters, pirates, spies, and other assorted evildoers. Action-packed cartoon serials like "Mickey Mouse Outwits the Phantom Blot" (1939) and "The Nazi Submarine" (1943) left no doubt that Mickey was the star, and his sillier friends strictly supporting players. Gottfredson, who took over from Walt and Ub Iwerks in 1929, worked on the strip in various capacities for more than forty-five years. And as he himself admitted in 1975, "the peak in the strip probably was around the early 1940s." It was in these strips, not the animated films of the 1940s, that the true spirit of Mickey Mouse could be found.

Despite taking a backseat to his comrades, Mickey still had the last word come D-Day. The password for the Allies who stormed the beach at Normandy to crush the German army was M-I-C-K-E-Y M-O-U-S-E!

ABOVE: Excerpt from the "Mickey Mouse and the Pirate Submarine" continuous adventure format comic. The strip offers a rare look at Mickey on the front lines, and gives a nod to the public's fascination with the peculiar machinery and harebrained inventors in popular science fiction of the time.

BELOW: "Mighty Minnie" insignia on a World War II matchbook

81

WOODSHOP MICKEY

In the 1940s, Mickey Mouse was a popular image in school workshops; and many a father at his garage or cellar workshop created wood cutouts taken from the die-cut shop patterns published in *Popular Mechanics* or *Modern Mechanix* magazines, of Mickey as bookends, stand-up silent butlers, ashtrays, endtables, doorstops, decorative plaques, garden scarecrows, and a variety of other household objects. The handmade and hand-painted wooden jigsaw cutouts are sometimes very accurate likenesses of Mickey Mouse, while some are more primitive in their execution, expressing an artistic license that brings a certain charm to the subject. These homemade Mickeys may still be found at Americana folk-art shows, right alongside quilts, weathervanes, embroidered pillows, and hand-hooked rugs.

"I fondly remember my father using a buzz saw to construct a freestanding magazine rack for me to house my collection of *Action Comic* books and *Modern Screen* movie magazines. After the final finish, my father headed for the corner hardware store where he bought a decal appliqué to dress up the piece: an image of a smiling Mickey standing in a field and holding a flower."—*Robert Heide*

CITIZEN MICKEY

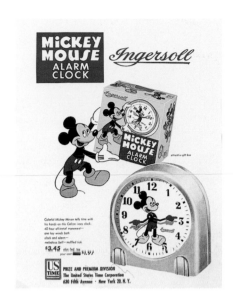

BIRTHDAY TIME

To celebrate Mickey's twentieth birthday in 1948, Ingersoll produced a Mickey Mouse Birthday collection of ten Disney watches with radium dials that glowed in the dark. Each watch sold for $6.95. The Big Birthday Box featured nine characters focusing on Mickey, who is holding a three-tiered birthday cake. When Mickey reached adulthood at twenty-one in 1949, Ingersoll produced an ivory Celcon plastic Mickey Mouse alarm clock and continued the birthday box in a different lineup, selling for a dollar more. The 1949 package came in the shape of a cake "with real candles that light" and included a "sterling silver ring" and a bright red ballpoint pen with a decal of Mickey on it.

ABOVE: *Radium dial "glow in the dark" wristwatch celebrates Mickey's twentieth birthday.*

ABOVE RIGHT: *Advertisement for the Celcon ivory Ingersoll Mickey Mouse alarm clock, 1949*

OPPOSITE: *Mickey the family mouse graces the cover of a 1940s school reader.*

With the conclusion of the war in 1945, things slowly began to get back to normal for the world and Mickey Mouse. Mickey had clearly settled down into his no-swearing, no-drinking, no-smoking, no-nonsense persona. He had established himself as a studio figurehead as well as worked his way into the hearts of millions across the globe. "Now he's Mikki Maus in Russia, Miki Kuchi in Japan, Miguel Ratoncito in Spanish-speaking countries, Michel Souris in France, and Topolino in Italy," said Walt.

85

MICKEY FOR SALE

From a variety of companies, Mickey made his way into the American home as wallpaper, rugs, radios like the Emerson Art Deco model, ceramics, pottery pieces, dishware, glass tumblers, Noritake and bisque figurine knickknacks, silverware, lithographed sheet-metal wastepaper baskets, breadboxes, children's eating trays, metal flowerpots, cake covers, pet-food platters, ceramic Mickey planters, cookie jars, ashtrays, and salt and pepper shakers.

86

Mickey stars in the second segment of Fun and Fancy Free (1947): Mickey and the Beanstalk.

"My husband always loved Mickey Mouse and he always had to have it in the White House." —Eleanor Roosevelt

Mickey did land a plum role in the Disney feature *Fun and Fancy Free* in 1947, where he regained some of his youthful pluck as the hero of "Mickey and the Beanstalk." The first-rate production was Mickey's story all the way, although Goofy and Donald were along to back him up. In the handful of Mickey shorts that followed the war, such as *Mickey's Delayed Date* (1947), *Mickey Down Under* (1948), and *Mickey and the Seal* (1948), he is the smiling suburban everyman, coping with household problems or taking a vacation accompanied by his dog. (If one were to judge by the amount of screen-time afforded them, it may be more accurate to say that Pluto is on vacation, accompanied by his mouse). None of this inertia seemed to affect Mickey merchandise sales, however, and by the end of the decade, nearly six million Mickey Mouse watches had been sold.

CHAPTER 3

THE
COMEBACK
KID

TRAP TIME

According to the Gallup Audience Research Institute, by the end of the 1940s, the American public ranked Donald Duck as its favorite cartoon character, followed by Bugs Bunny and Mickey Mouse. Walt marveled at the poll results, which came at a time when Mickey's days seemed to be clearly numbered. "Five years off the screen and he still rates third! Is there any star in Hollywood with a public that loyal?"

LEFT: Mickey settles in for the night in this storybook illustration.

ABOVE & OPPOSITE: Animation of Mickey pulling up a fish (above) and poster (opposite) from The Simple Things (1953), Mickey's last short for thirty years

"Mickey's our problem child. He's so much of an institution that we're limited in what we can do with him. Mickey must always be sweet and lovable. What can you do with such a leading man?" —Walt Disney

ABOVE: *Mickey settles in to his suburbanite role. Animation of Mickey from Plutopia (1951)*

But the public's devotion to Mickey wasn't enough. From the beginning, Walt had served as Mickey's ultimate storyman, character builder, and casting agent. His idea bank was just about empty. Mickey appeared in five films between 1951 and 1953, and in every one Pluto upstaged him. With the release of his 118th short, *The Simple Things*, Mickey quietly retired from films, just shy of his twenty-fifth birthday. By now even his comic strip, the last bastion of the more dynamic, original Mickey, had reverted from serialized stories to a gag-a-day format, falling into the same suburban rut as his final cartoon shorts. Aside from the continued strong and steady sales of Mickey merchandise, it appeared that after a quarter of a century, Mickey Mouse had finally outlived his usefulness. "I'm tired of Mickey now," Walt Disney admitted in 1951. "For him it's definitely trap time. The Mouse and I have been together for about twenty-two years. That's long enough for any association."

92

By the start of the 1950s, Mickey had transformed from an intrepid adventurer to more a sedate suburbanite who rarely ventures beyond his own neighborhood. This comic, dated January 3, 1949, features Eega Beeva, the "little man of the future" who first appeared in the Mickey Mouse comic strip in 1947.

In the 1950s, paint-by-numbers became a popular pastime. Hobbyists could reproduce everything from colorful clowns and quaint landscapes to da Vinci's *Mona Lisa* and Gainsborough's *Blue Boy* and *Lady Innes* (a.k.a. "Pinky"). Animation art ranked high among popular paint-by-number subjects, and fans could "create" their very own Mickeys to hang on their walls.

93

ABOVE: *A man and his mouse. This image adorns the stairway of Walt Disney Feature Animation in Burbank.*

Walt's harsh words belied his true feelings for his brainchild. After all, Mickey Mouse had put Walt Disney on the map, and Walt never forgot it. *New York Times* film critic Frank Nugent once inquired about Mickey Mouse's earnings. "What's he make a year—what's he made in all?" Walt simply replied, "Me." The sun may have set on Mickey's Hollywood career, but the postwar boom led Walt to believe that Mickey would again have his time in the sun.

MOUSE IN THE HOUSE

Black-and-white television sets entered living rooms across the land in the 1950s. Referred to by skeptical Americans as "that little blue box" because of the gray-bluish glare that emanated from the early tube sets, the new technology, which originally previewed at the 1939 New York World's Fair, had arrived. One commentator of the day referred to TV entertainment emanating out of "the box" as Tired Vaudeville, because of the number of unemployed vaudevillians, circus clowns, dogs, and high-wire acts who suddenly were regulars on live television. Walt immediately recognized the potential of the new medium.

Unlike other Hollywood producers who condemned television as the death knell of theater, Walt saw it as the perfect publicity vehicle. "The public has been my friend. The public discovered Mickey Mouse before the critics and before the theatrical people," Walt said explaining his reasons for going into TV. "Television is going to be my way of going direct to the public, bypassing the others who can sit there and be the judge on the bench." Fearful that Disney would employ the film talent of other studios in his new venture; Hollywood executives accused him of selling out. But Walt intended to do just that: sell his upcoming ideas to a receptive audience, skipping the middleman.

ABOVE: *Mickey Mouse button commemorating the 1939 New York World's Fair*

BELOW: *Artwork created for the "Walt Disney Christmas Show," one of the earliest Disney television productions. The special, which promoted Peter Pan, aired on December 25, 1951.*

94

Look Magazine visual time line illustrates the history of Walt Disney Productions up to the conception of Disneyland.

One Hour in Wonderland, Walt's first foray into America's living rooms aired on NBC, Christmas Day, 1950. The holiday special was a thinly veiled ploy to whet the public's appetite for his upcoming feature Alice in Wonderland and determine television's potential impact on box-office sales. As part of the core entertainment, Walt brought in his trusted friends, Mickey and pals. Walt couldn't have predicted better results. Twenty million viewers tuned in—a whopping ninety percent of the nation's television audience.

Syndicated columnist John Crosby wrote of the special: "[It] must have struck despair into the hearts of most of the people who earn a living in the medium. There is nothing in television even remotely comparable to Mickey Mouse, Donald Duck, Dopey, Goofy, Pluto, and the rest of them. And there isn't likely to be, ever."

Walt would repeat the formula the following year, again to rave reviews. With the experimental phase behind him, he knew the

95

Sunday color comic dated February 21, 1951, featuring the everyday goings-on of the domestic mouse

time was ripe to plan for a larger television presence. The timing dovetailed perfectly with his plans to introduce the world to his fantastical family park, and to reach the newly bloated population of kids—seventy-three million—who had yet to discover the magic of Mickey.

For years Walt considered building an amusement park across the street from his Burbank studio and calling it Mickey Mouse Park. But Walt had big ideas and the small tract of land could not hold them. By 1952, Walt finally came up with the official name of his Mickey Mouse Park: Disneyland. As part of the masterful financing plans for the park, Walt and his brother Roy O. Disney

96

ABOVE: *Each episode of the Mickey Mouse Club began with an animated segment winding up with Donald's bang of the club gong, with mixed fallout. Here Donald averts disaster by playing a triangle instead.*

BELOW: *Bandleader Mickey marches to the club song.*

sold the struggling ABC network on two innovative TV series: a prime-time show called *Disneyland*, and a five-times-a-week children's hour called *The Mickey Mouse Club*.

The format for the kiddie variety show centered on the idea of a club that would follow in the footsteps of the children's Saturday movie-matinee Mickey Mouse Clubs popular in the early thirties. Each show opened with emcee Mickey, who introduced the theme for that day: Fun with Music Day, Guest Star Day, Anything Can Happen Day, Circus Day, Talent Round-up Day. The grand finale featured a Mousekartoon from the studio's vaults. Many of the shorts screened on the show had not been seen by an audience since their initial theatrical release in the thirties.

97

On October 3, 1955, the program premiered on television, opening with the announcement: "Walt Disney and Mickey Mouse present *The Mickey Mouse Club*." The show, with its jamboree of songs, stories, games, movie shorts, Hardy Boys serials, Newsreel Specials, Mystery Series, and animal adventures, became a hit with kids—and adults—all over the country. Within a year, nearly 14.5 million viewers were hooked—a testament to the new precedence the show set in children's programming. Walt had a stroke of genius when he appointed former Mickey Mouse comic-strip gag writer, Bill Walsh, as the show's producer; together they decided that the club should be represented by talented children. Thousands of hopeful kids auditioned, but only twenty-four made the final cut to be official Mouseketeers. After the second season, fifteen new Mouseketeers joined in the fun, bringing the total to thirty-nine. Adult costar Jimmie Dodd wrote more than thirty of the *Mickey Mouse Club* songs, including the Club's theme song, "The Mickey Mouse Club March." *The Mickey Mouse Club* aired daily from five to six P.M., but eventually adopted a half-hour format maintained through September 25, 1959.

"Everyone who regularly watches THE MICKEY MOUSE CLUB television show is automatically a member of the Mickey Mouse Club and a Mouseketeer First Class in Good Standing!"—Walt Disney

98

Mouseketeers don felt mouse-ear caps.

OPPOSITE: *The Mickey Mouse Club logo*

"The circle always points to the single most vital aspect of life—it's ultimate wholeness."—Psychologist Carl Jung, analyzing Mickey Mouse,

observing that his head was comprised of a trinity of circles

ABOVE & BELOW: *The gag in Karnival Kid (below) that Williams credited as his inspiration for the mouse-eared caps was originally used by Ub Iwerks in one of the Oswald the Lucky Rabbit shorts (above).*

ABOVE RIGHT: *The Mickey Mouse Clubhouse set from the show*

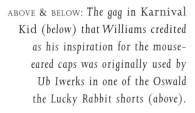

Coming on the heels of the former radio star Howdy Doody and the first network kids' show on CBS, *Captain Kangaroo*, *The Mickey Mouse Club* launched children's television into a whole new dimension unleashing a fan-club craze. "Mouseketeer" gear flooded the merchandise marketplace including a "Walt Disney Official Mickey Mouse Hat" designed by "Big Mooseketeer" Roy Williams. The black skull-cap featured two round Mickey ears and a Mouseketeer logo patch with a pink-faced Mickey set in the center. Williams credited his inspiration for the caps to a gag in *The Karnival Kid* (1929), in which Mickey lifts off the top of his head to Minnie as if it were a hat.

100

The MOUSEKETEER "MOUSECAP"

#800 — Mickey Mouse

#802 — Minnie Mouse

The ubiquitous cap sold in stores throughout the United States for 69¢ and became a primary symbol of 1950s Mickey Mouse popular culture. Children who wore these funky hats to school were proud to be known as official members of the club. Mouseketeer games, photo albums, comb-and-brush sets, toothbrushes, roller skates, toy TV cameras, Mickey night lights, playhouses, scooters, wagons, radios, pinback buttons, kites, Mouse-Getars, activity books, comics, and even shoe polish sold like hot cakes, competing with the top TV merchandise of Roy Rogers, Gene Autry, and Hopalong Cassidy.

As spokesmouse for the inspirational and educational show, Mickey became an authority figure that children—and parents— could trust. When the honest Mouse stood behind General Foods, Standard Oil, National Biscuit Company, and National Dairy

101

Products, consumers bought his word—and the goods. Countless companies clamored to get Mickey, whose endorsements were worth their weight in gold, to be their salesman. No small wonder then that liquor companies, cigarette manufacturers, and pharmaceutical companies put their bids in for the mighty salesman. But the Mouse kept to his high standards and refused to sell any products that didn't jibe with his wholesome outlook.

According to author Richard Schickel, during this decade, Mickey "appeared on five thousand different items, which had contributed a quarter of a billion dollars to the gross national product." From Movie-Star Mouse to Television Star, Mickey had become known in the industry as "The Comeback Kid." Not bad for a little guy who started off the decade as mousetrap bait.

"Who's the leader of the Club that's made for you and me?
M–I–C–K–E–Y M–O–U–S–E!"

LEFT: *Suede Mouseketeer wallet sold at Disneyland in the 1950s*

OPPOSITE: *Mouseketeers vest and mask set in original package*

103

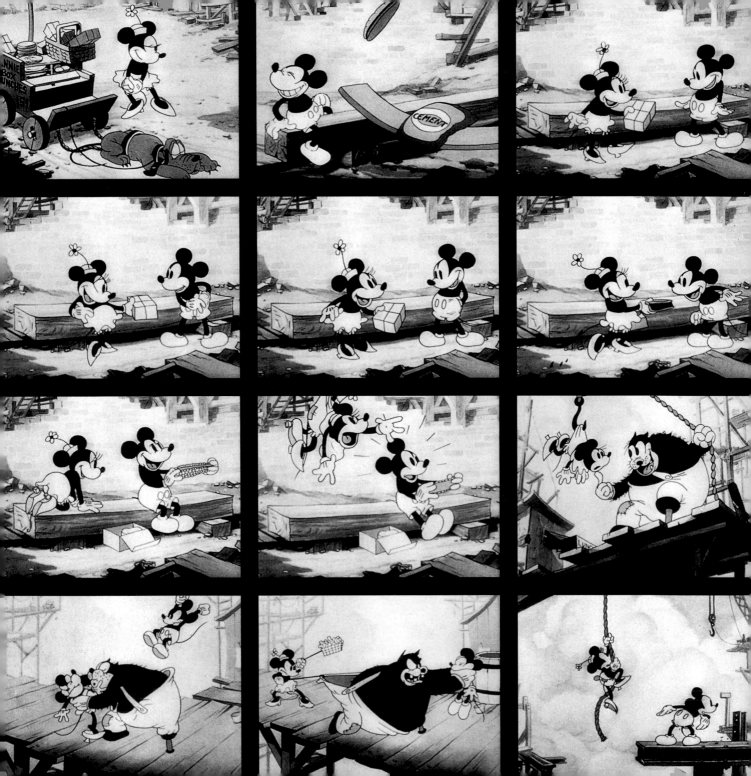

A new generation of children was introduced to the cartoon mouse through watching his shorts on the Mickey Mouse Club. In Building a Building (1933), Minnie offers Mickey a lunchbox from her cart after his foreman, Pete, steals his. Pete tries to kidnap Minnie, but she and Mickey outsmart their foe and then ride off into the sunset as partners in Minnie's business.

ABOVE: *Walt Disney enlisted Imagineer Herb Ryman to create concept drawings of Disneyland for his proposal to get the banks to back his fantastic venture.*

RIGHT AND OPPOSITE: *Walk-around characters were present at opening of Disneyland, July 17, 1955 (right), and would evolve considerably through the years.*

A WALK IN THE PARK

In the very first episode of *Disneyland*, Walt introduced his new park uttering his now-famous words: "I hope we never lose sight of one thing—that it was all started by a mouse." Disneyland park opened in July 1955, and drew one million guests within seven weeks; five million within fifteen months. The event signified a growth spurt for Mickey—about five feet. Mickey had leapt off the page, transforming from 2-D to 3-D. For the first time, children visiting "The Happiest Place on Earth" could have their picture taken with a "real" Mickey Mouse.

"Mickey's transformation from the 2-D to 3-D worlds was natural, except for the design, of course," says Imagineer John Hench. "It is actually astonishing that Mickey held his identity. Making him a real, live character represented a violent shift that violated the head-to-body proportion [of the 2-D character]."

The costumes for opening day were borrowed from the Ice Capades. Mickey didn't actually become a staple in the park until a few years later. "After a time," Hench continues, "we made our own costumes for the walk-around characters. Of course, we got better at it as we went along. For example, we found smaller people [to wear the costumes] who didn't distort the image so much. The first characters weren't that great, I guess."

ABOVE: *Walt Disney delivers his speech during the opening day ceremonies at Disneyland.*

OVERLEAF: *Mickey, Minnie, the Three Little Pigs, Chip and Dale join with the "Dickens Carolers" during the Christmas season at Disneyland.*

106

ABOVE: *Walk-around characters pose in front of Sleeping Beauty Castle at Disneyland.*

BELOW: *Each year, Disneyland was host to a Christmas parade called "Fantasy on Parade" that featured many Disney characters.*

The costumes have continued to evolve since those first characters walked through Disneyland. The wizards at Imagineering constantly modify the costumes. "We are working on one that will be much more expressive."

Mickey was more than just a celebrity in the park. From the moment guests came through the gates, a blooming Mickey adorning the floral bed below Main Street Station greeted them. Mickey's presence in the park continues to remind guests of who is at the heart of it all—from a topiary Mickey near It's a Small World to decorative ironwork in New Orleans Square.

110

"Mickey Mouse, as always, is the national hero.
His likeness hangs in the windows of homes, in the shops,
on baby buggies, in private cars, taxis and buses."

—Mike Connelly, reporting from Italy in 1953

Model sheet of comic strip poses, 1959

CHAPTER 4

COUNTER-
CULTURAL
POP STAR

The themes and costumes of the comic strips continued to reinforce the humanizing trend in designing Mickey Mouse.
A daily strip from October 17, 1965, places Mickey in the role of a middle-class family man.

114 "My parents always gave us kids, myself, and my three sisters, Mickey Mouse birthday parties in the fifties and sixties, including Mickey hats, paper napkins, paper plates, a Mickey table cover and—yes—a Mickey Mouse birthday cake with a music box inside. For my tenth Mickey Mouse birthday party, they took me for the first time to Disneyland; and I almost fainted when I got to meet the 'live' Mickey Mouse—in person."

—Carol Tooker, Barnegat, New Jersey, grade-school teacher

ABOVE: *Artist Ray Johnson in his own hand-painted Mickey Mouse jacket*

RIGHT: *Pen-and-ink drawing of Mickey Mouse by Ray Johnson*

PEACE, LOVE, AND MICKEY

In the sixties Mickey became more than the fashion statement he'd come to be in previous years. He became a powerful symbol of love. Wearing a Mickey watch or T-shirt to a Love-in or a Be-in seemed to be "right on." "Do your own thing," the message of the sixties' hippies and outcasts, exactly sums up just what Mickey always did.

The decade of the 1960s embraced Pop, Op, and Psychedelic art; and a period of under-thirty counterculture took hold. It was a visual decade, fueled by a spirit of rebellion that created a love revolution, backed up by the Beatles who proclaimed to the world that "All You Need Is Love." The new hippie underground, led by self-proclaimed guru Timothy Leary, turned on, tuned in, and dropped out with mind-opening drugs, such as LSD and marijuana, which made the experience of color and motion, and thus of animated art, more intense. To the rest of the nation, Mickey appeared to have "dropped out" as well, maintaining the lowest visibility of his career. Other than occasional television appearances on *The Mickey Mouse Club* reruns and *Walt Disney's Wonderful World of Color*, fans had to either search the newspaper and comic books or go to Anaheim, California, to see Mickey Mouse. But the real place to find Mickey alive and well was underground.

RIGHT: *Disney artist Ward Kimball's tongue-in-cheek caricature illustrates just how far Mickey had come by the 1970s.*

PRECEDING SPREAD: *Mickey wears many hats, including Charlie Chaplin's (lower right), in this Colorforms brochure for the Mickey Mouse Puppetforms activity game.*

ABOVE: *"Funny World" pen-and-ink drawing of Minnie and Mickey and their Barnyard Pals as windup toys by artist John Fawcett*

OPPOSITE: *Ray Johnson collage of Mickey Mouse*

116

Mickey Mouse entered the realm of high art when Pop artists such as Andy Warhol, Claes Oldenburg, Roy Lichtenstein, and others chose Mickey as an important American icon for subject matter in their artwork. Some, like John Fawcett, who also collects Mickeyana, used Mickey as the primary subject for their art. Ray Johnson created intricate collages, many featuring Mickey Mouse in the overall assemblages. Best known for his New York Correspondence School, Johnson included many images of Mickey as an aspect of his collage and Mail Art, now in the collections of many art collectors and distinguished museums, such as the Whitney Museum in New York and the Victoria and Albert Museum in London.

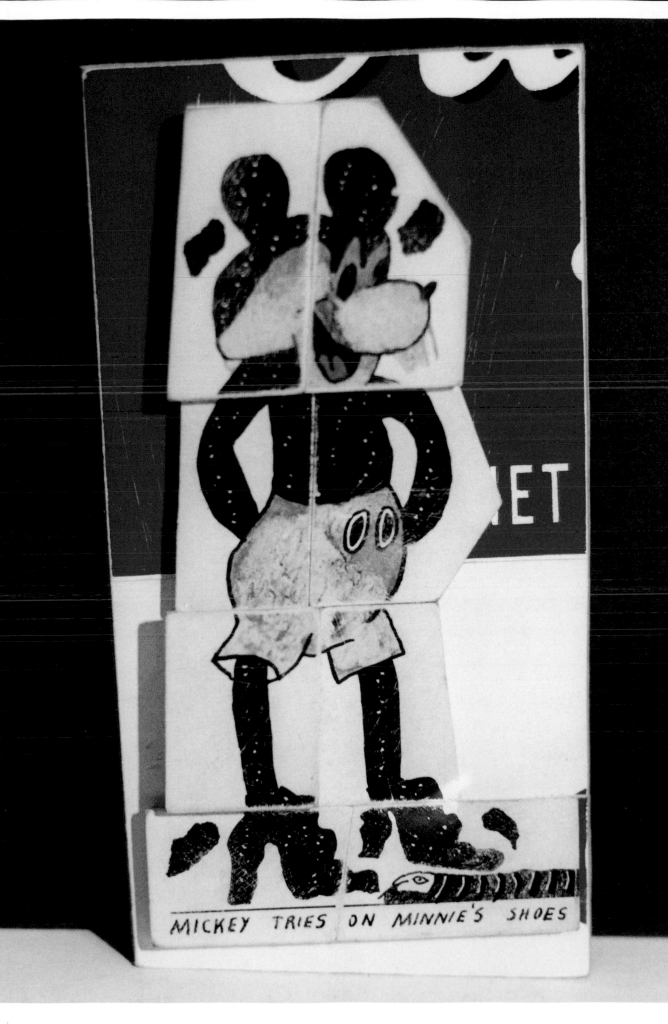

"Mickey Mouse is my favorite actor! Minnie Mouse is my favorite actress! My very own favorite personal hero is Walt Disney!" —Andy Warhol

ABOVE: *Mickey Mouse "turnabout" cookie jar features Minnie on the other side.*

ABOVE RIGHT: *Mickey Mouse Beetleware mug*

OPPOSITE: *Andy Warhol's "Myths: Mickey Mouse"—part of his series that also includes Uncle Sam, Superman, and Santa Claus—enhanced the Mouse's icon status and gave him a firm place in the world of Pop Art.*

Hippies on a visual "trip" plumbed flea markets and antique shows in search of a lost and disappearing America even as the country welcomed in the new technological age. Life Magazine reported that hippies began wearing original 1930s Ingersoll Mickey Mouse watches they picked up in their travels, and noted that they preferred the early, more mischievous, rodentlike imp-mouse to the latter-day rounded or pear-shaped humanoid Mickey developed in the 1940s and 1950s.

Andy Warhol was but one of the sixties superstar Pop artists who embraced Mickey Mouse and went on a search for Art Deco and other lost treasures, such as the Mickey Mouse Turnabout cookie jar, one of his favorite collectibles. Unable to cope with what Warhol called "The Plastic Inevitable" and others labeled the "Era of the Cheap Disposable," many people felt the need to look back, seeking comfort and refuge in the past. A craze for the 1930s, the Depression era, took hold.

119

FLEA-MARKET MICKEY

A Mickey Mouse Revival was underway, making Mickey as popular as he had been in the era of the Great Depression. Michael Malce became one of the first dealers to bring early Mickey Mouse memorabilia into the forefront of the antiques marketplace of the early 1960s. He and partner Kenny Kneitel, Out-of-the-Inkwell artist Max Fleischer's grandson, set up shop in an antique boutique called Fandango, which helped set the stage for the Mickey Mouse memorabilia revival and nurtured a following of new Mickey collectors.

BELOW: *The 1934 Ingersoll Mickey Mouse wristwatch enjoyed a renaissance in the sixties.*

"In the late sixties, after all the assassinations and the devastation of the Vietnam War, something inside of me seemed to want to go back to Mickey. It was at an open-air flea market that I found the same Ingersoll Mickey Mouse wristwatch I had had as a child. I had to own it again."—Henry Mazzeo, advertising copywriter

120

Mickey's fortieth birthday came during one of America's most turbulent years. Public opinion on the escalating Vietnam War was growing more heated, race relations were reaching a boiling point, and the nation endured the assassinations of the Reverend Martin Luther King, Jr., and Senator Robert F. Kennedy. Mickey's birthday provided some relief, and some surprises: when a watch picturing Mickey Mouse returned from a decade-long hiatus in production, adults bought as many as children did.

In the October 25, 1968, Life magazine issue on the occasion of Mickey Mouse's fortieth birthday, the focus was on the hippie counterculture's obsession with the early 1930s mischievous Mickey Mouse. This went hand in hand with a group of collectors and artists who were gathering up the old stuff from flea markets and attics that came to be known as "Mickey Mouse Memorabilia" or "Disneyana." One article featured aficionado Mel Birnkrant along with fellow Mickey collectors Ernest Trova and Robert Lesser, as forerunners signaling the surge of the retro-revival Mickey movement, which favored the more impish rapscallion mouse. In another report, the Horn & Hardart Restaurant chain of Automats offered a "rodent-fetish special"—a free piece of cheesecake to anyone wearing a Mickey Mouse watch like the Mod Ingersoll-Timex worn by Wally Schirra aboard the Apollo 7 spacecraft that orbited Earth in 1968.

BELOW: *Vintage Mickey collectible with Indian headdress and tomahawk*

OPPOSITE: *Mickey Mouse Scatter Ball game produced in 1934 by Marks Brothers of Boston, Massachusetts*

With Mickey Mouse watches back in vogue, Ingersoll-Timex created a new version of their own to meet the demand. The watches sold for $12.95 each; the total production, meant to last a year, sold out before the end of the first month in the market. Astronauts Gene Cernan wore one such watch during his moonwalk on the Apollo 10 mission in May 1969. Celebrities Johnny Carson and Carol Burnett showed off their new status-symbol Mickey timepieces on TV.

Ted Hake is yet another pioneer of the Mickey Mouse merchandise collecting craze. He recognized that Mickey items would be the wampum of collectibles as the Mouse became the cartoon-character leader of the expanding Pop-culture movement that was sweeping the "new" antiques marketplace. Collecting started at a furiously competitive pace, ultimately driving prices upward, particularly in the area of all things Mickey. Hake's catalogs offered Disneyana of all kinds, as well as political campaign pinback buttons, sports items, ship, railroad, aviation, and automobile mementos, early radio premiums, advertising ephemera, comics, Big Little Books, tin toys, Cowboyana, movie-related materials, and TV collectibles; but always at the top of the auction at hand was Mickey. Some Mickey items fell into the highest category, "$2000 and over," because of their rarity and desirability.

"In the 1930s, Disney licensed over fifty thousand different objects worldwide—I want them all!"—Mel Birnkrant

GOOD-BYE, WALT

In December of 1966 Mickey was on the front page of newspapers around the world, but for the saddest reason: the death of his creator, Walt Disney. On the cover of *Paris Match* a bereft Mickey Mouse wept at the loss of his beloved creator.

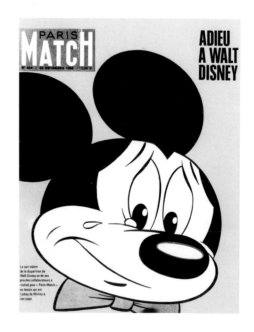

124

By the end of the decade, Mickey had become an established icon of a new generation. The re-release of *Fantasia* in 1969 reintroduced Sorcerer Mickey as a true star. The film took off as an underground–above-ground hit. The youth-culture crowd, some of whom popped sugar cubes laced with LSD while watching the film, exclaimed that they really "Got it!" Young people identified with the conceptual images on the screen and sought out the film's creators, wondering if they had taken drugs while they were making it. "Yes, I was on drugs," animator Art Babbitt admitted, "Ex-Lax and Pepto Bismol!"

BELOW: Mickey slides down a cucumber on a Mel Birnkrant designed seed packet.

OPPOSITE: Mickey is conspicuously absent from the poster created for the 1969 re-release of Fantasia.

"If you can stand aside and learn to laugh at your own foibles and anger the way you laugh at a Mickey Mouse cartoon, it can help you to realize the fundamental absurdity of everything in the universe."

—B. K. Joy, Shiva Baba follower

125

ABOVE: Logo for the Mickey & Company fashion line

BELOW: Mickey Mouse Nitelite in its original packaging

OPPOSITE: In the summer of 1973, Lincoln Center hosted the Walt Disney 50th Anniversary Film Retrospective at Alice Tully Hall in New York. Program commentators and hosts were Christopher Finch and John Culhane. The July 10, 1973, New York Times headline declared "Disney Festival Offers Nostalgia for Old and Déjà Vu for Young."

MICKEY REVIVAL

The popularity of Mickey Mouse as a cultural icon at the end of the sixties continued into the 1970s, with Sotheby's first "Disneyana" auction in 1972, the first book devoted to Disney collectibles in 1974, and, by the end of the decade, a new fashion line, Mickey & Company, which offered high-priced adult clothing and accessories to an ever-growing market. Museums and galleries began re-examining the Mouse again with an intensity not seen since Mickey's heyday of the 1930s.

The word *camp*, borrowed from the gay subculture in a celebrated 1964 essay by Susan Sontag, referred in the seventies to the high–low tongue-in-cheek aspect of mass-produced Art Deco, including Mickey Mouse himself, as well as 1930s hotel orchestra music, which had been referred to as Mickey Mouse music. At the same time, many scholars, artists, and historians of popular culture treated camp quite seriously. Like famed illustrators and commercial artists Maxfield Parrish and Norman Rockwell, Disney and Mickey, with the help of the Pop Art movement, had begun to enter the high-end art market. Studio cels and Mickeyana were showing up at top auction houses like Sotheby's and Parke-Bernet, with bids reaching unexpectedly high levels.

128

A metal wastepaper basket, sold at Woolworth's in the seventies during the oil crisis that bedeviled the Carter administration, depicts Mickey and Minnie with an empty fuel can hitchhiking beside their stalled auto.

Stephen Jay Gould, Professor of Zoology and Geology at Harvard University, believed that Mickey Mouse actually reverted into a more infantile state over the years, eventually looking more like one of his nephews, Morty and Ferdie. In an article entitled "Mickey Mouse Meets Konrad Lorenz" in *Natural History Magazine* (May 1979), Gould claimed that Disney artists transformed Mickey, acting on an unconscious discovery of Konrad Lorenz's belief that the facial features of juvenility trigger "innate releasing mechanisms," thus eliciting powerful emotional responses from adults (and children).

A wave of nostalgic yearning for a fun and simple time had developed. Weary of the dangerous and complicated present and fearful of an uncertain future, Americans began celebrating the past. And what better example of simplicity, fun, and the past than Mickey Mouse? New merchandise began to feature the "pie-eye" Mickey of the 1930s almost as much as the "human eye" Mouse into which he had evolved. The middle-aged embraced Mickey, seeing him as a comforting symbol from their past, whereas the revolutionary youth saw something in Mickey with which they could identify: a rebellious nature combined with a sweetly confident naïveté.

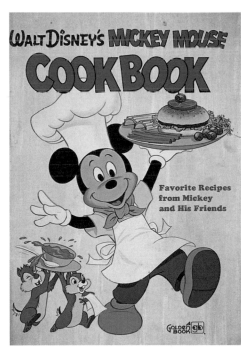

In the 1950s, Disney adopted an increasingly infantile character design for Mickey, as noted by Stephen Jay Gould, and seen in this 1953 Mickey Mouse Birthday Party comic book by Dell Publishers (upper right). The more childlike Mickey persisted through the 1970s, as on the cover of the 1975 Mickey Mouse Cookbook (right). Mickey's design did begin to resemble that of his nephews: Morty and Ferdie buy travel tickets in this illustration from Walt Disney's "Mystery in Disneyville" Golden Book, 1949 (bottom).

129

COLORFORMS

Mel Birnkrant joined the Colorforms Co. of Ramsey, New Jersey, in 1970 as their creative director, and remained in that post until 1985, designing a series of boxed games and other products, mostly issued in 1978, that used the early 1930s image of Mickey Mouse in a way that had not been used on a commercial product since the Depression era.

CARROT
IMPROVED CHANTENAY
Net Wt.
2 g.
59¢
PRODUCE

DAISY
DAISY GLORIOSA   SINGLE MIXED COLORS
Net Wt.
600 mg.   59¢

WALT DISNEY WONDERFUL WORLD OF GARDENING

In 1976, Mel Birnkrant designed seed packets with colorful graphic images of Mickey and friends. The stick-in-the-ground, all-weather vinyl row markers featured Minnie holding a zinnia, Mickey hauling a cartload of giant radishes, and the like.

132

PUMPKIN
JACK-O-LANTERN
Net Wt.
4 g.

59¢

WALT DISNEY WONDERFUL WORLD OF GARDENING

ZINNIA
CALIFORNIA GIANTS   MIXED COLORS
Net Wt.
900 mg.

59¢

WALT DISNEY WONDERFUL WORLD OF GARDENING

SUPERSTAR STATUS

Walt Disney World opened in 1971, and Mickey Mouse took center stage in one of the most popular initial attractions, the Mickey Mouse Revue, in which an Audio-Animatronics® Mickey led a chorus of Disney characters in a medley of classic Disney songs. The park—and Mickey—would greet fifty million guests by 1976. Meanwhile, on the West Coast, Disneyland drew ten million visitors in 1970, and the following year welcomed its 100-millionth guest.

Mickey Mouse was on hand to help celebrate the continuation of Walt's dream, the opening of Walt Disney World: on a postcard (above left); with Minnie on a commemorative tile (left); and with Roy O. Disney on opening day of the Magic Kingdom at Walt Disney World, October 1, 1971 (opposite).

OVERLEAF: "Floral Mickey" freshens up in preparation for Walt Disney World Magic Kingdom visitors.

136

In 1972, veteran Disney animator Ward Kimball produced *The Mouse Factory*, a syndicated television series that blended clips from Disney cartoons with a celebrity host to explore a topic like vacations or dancing. One of the most memorable shows, hosted by former Mouseketeer Annette Funicello, focused solely on Mickey. And in 1977, an all-new version of *The Mickey Mouse Club* reminiscent of the 1950s show, appeared in fifty-four broadcast markets. Mickey capped the decade with a fiftieth-birthday celebration in 1978, which attracted unprecedented media and consumer attention.

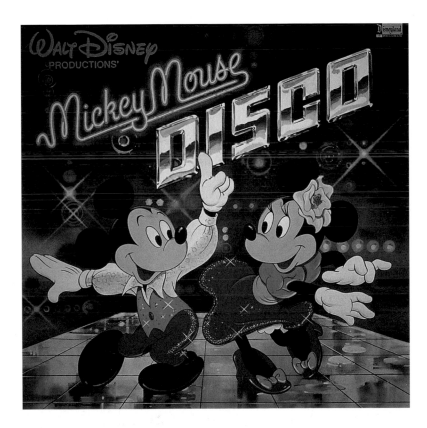

LEFT: *Mickey and Minnie draw upon their long history of experience as dance partners (above) to jump into the Disco craze that sweeps the nation, on this Mickey Mouse Disco album cover.*

141

OPPOSITE: *Mickey's ticket to board his special fiftieth birthday train is punched by the conductor, animator and train enthusiast Ward Kimball.*

BIRTHDAY BOY

In December 1975, the Museum of Modern Art in New York showed a new film made by the Disney Studio called *Mickey's Birthday Party*, which traced the development of Mickey in his first sound film in 1928 through 1975. The film was hosted by Mickeyphile Gene London, who later specialized in the buying and selling of movie-star clothes.

The biggest Mickey Mouse birthday bash took place in 1978; all-year-long celebrations connected to Mickey's fiftieth birthday opened up in January with elaborate parades at both Disneyland and Walt Disney World. Television stations all across the United States aired $2 million worth of broadcast and print advertising in September and October including "Happy Birthday Mickey" clips. Mickey was a star attraction of the Macy's Thanksgiving Day Parade. Retailers received ten million "Happy Birthday Mickey" sweepstakes flyers in the mail. Mickey himself traveled cross-country aboard a special birthday train with animator Ward Kimball, attending stop-off ceremonies in Kansas City (November 14), Chicago (November 15), Washington, D. C. (November 17), and arriving in New York on November 18 to inaugurate a special new plaque in the lobby of the Broadway Theater, formerly the Colony Theater.

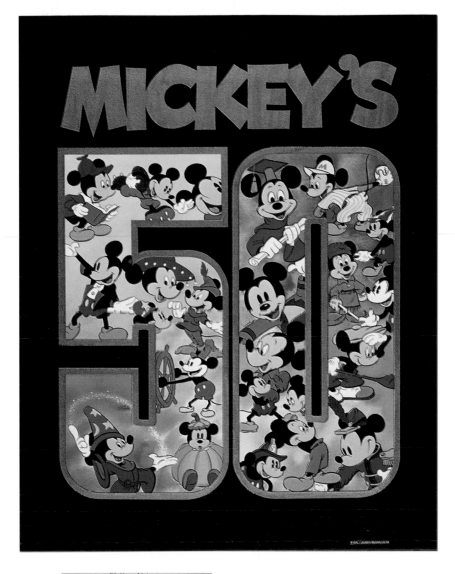

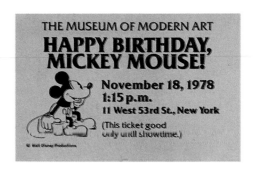

ABOVE: *Admission ticket for New York's Museum of Modern Art Mickey Mouse birthday party, November 18, 1978.*

LEFT: *Poster created to honor Mickey's fiftieth birthday showcases many of his most memorable roles.*

BELOW LEFT: *Catalog from the Library of Congress Exhibit, "Building a Better Mouse" held in Washington, D. C., in 1978.*

OPPOSITE: *"Official" Mickey Mouse portrait created by Disney artist John Hench for Mickey's fiftieth. Hench has created the "official" birthday portraits beginning with Mickey's twenty-fifth in 1953.*

Birthday celebrations culminated at the Museum of Modern Art with a showing of *Steamboat Willie* at noon Saturday, November 18, 1978, fifty years to the precise minute after the first appearance of the Mickey Mouse film at the Colony Theater in New York.

Life magazine celebrated Mickey Mouse's fiftieth year on its November, 1978 cover with a proud Mickey painting his own likeness into a continuously miniaturized infinity.

The Library of Congress mounted an exhibition in Washington, D. C., from November 21, 1978, to January 30, 1979, called "Building a Better Mouse" and included more than 120 rare and previously unseen examples from their collections.

146

ABOVE: *Birnkrant's Mouse-Eum Easter egg, lunchbox, and popcorn display at L. Bamberger's Department Store in Newark in 1973 (poster, opposite).*

BELOW: *The animated somersaulting neon Mickey Mouse clock from the collection of Mel Birnkrant.*

November 19, 1973, the day after Mickey's official birthday, New Jersey's largest and most prestigious department store opened its sixth annual Holiday Art Exhibit with the Mickey Mouse-eum, the highlight of the Christmas season. The floodgates had opened wide in terms of the serious collecting of Mickey Mouse memorabilia, as well as mass-produced items commemorating other comic characters of the 1930s Golden Age. Little Orphan Annie, Felix the Cat, Betty Boop, Bimbo, Buck Rogers, Dick Tracy, Spark Plug, Barney Google, Buster Brown, Maggie and Jiggs, Happy Hooligan, Skippy, Krazy Kat, and many more were now sought after with unrelenting frenzy.

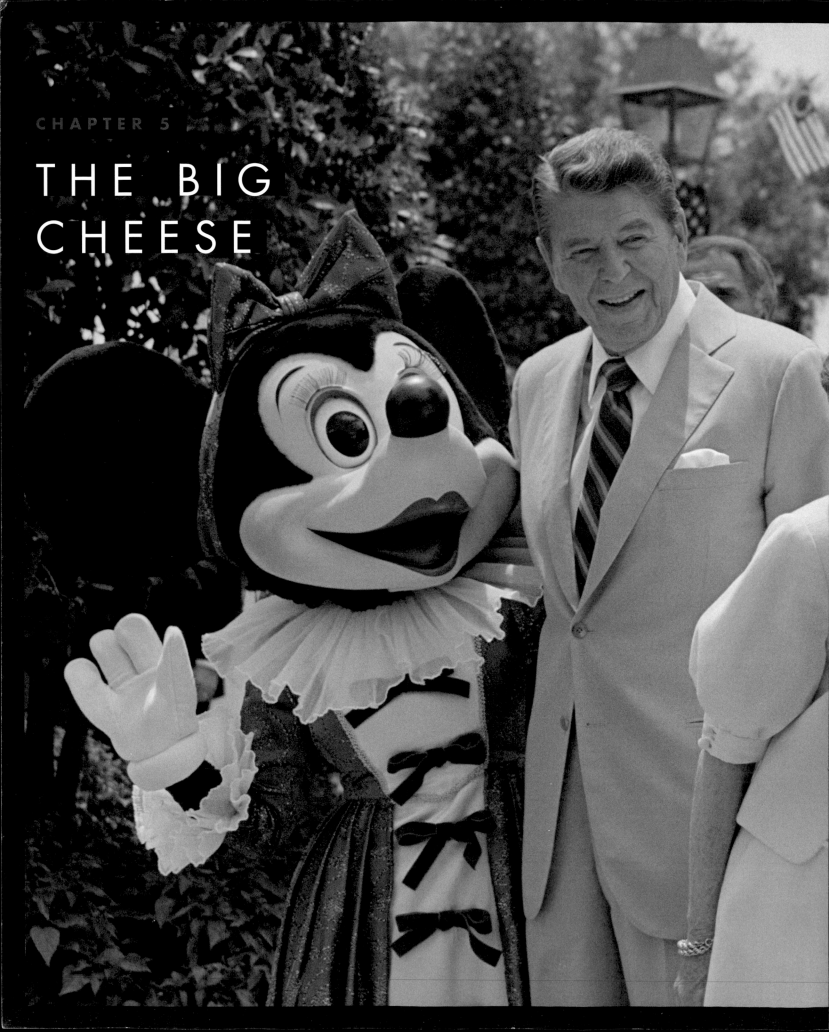

CHAPTER 5

THE BIG CHEESE

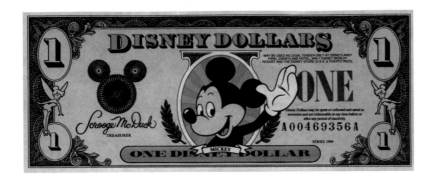

ABOVE: *Mickey Mouse embellishes the front of the Disney Dollar, legal tender in the theme parks and Disney Stores.*

RIGHT: *Animation drawings from Runaway Brain (1995)*

OPPOSITE: *Mickey Mouse dolls in a merchandise display in World Bazaar at Tokyo Disneyland*

PRECEDING PAGES: *First Lady Nancy Reagan kisses Mickey Mouse at Epcot in Walt Disney World as Minnie and President Reagan look on.*

RENAISSANCE MOUSE

For Mickey Mouse and his parent organization, the eighties felt a lot like one of Mickey's old-time cartoons: exciting action, followed by genuine danger, climaxing in a happy ending.

The action took place primarily in theme parks. Disneyland saw its 200-millionth guest in 1981, Walt Disney World its 300-millionth in 1989, and three entirely new parks opened their gates to the public: Epcot in 1982, Tokyo Disneyland the following year, and Disney-MGM Studios in 1989.

The expansion penetrated beyond the parks and into the home. Disney released its first batch of home video titles in 1980, including the compilation *On Vacation with Mickey Mouse and Friends*, and launched the Disney Channel on cable television in 1983. Programs such as *Mouseterpiece Theatre*, and in the nineties *Mouse Tracks* and *Quack Attack* revived the classic Disney cartoon shorts, including the earliest Mickeys, which hadn't been seen in three decades. Finally, the films that had created the legend had become readily accessible for new generations to discover. Mickey further enhanced his Disney Channel visibility by appearing on *Mousercise*, a children's exercise program, and in 1989, a new *Mickey Mouse Club* premiered.

For those who needed a Mickey fix in between trips to the parks or episodes on cable television, many needed to go no farther than the local mall; in 1987 the first Disney Store opened in Glendale, California. For the first time, outside the gates of Disneyland or Walt Disney World, a retail store offered exclusive lines of clothing, toys, housewares, books, audio, video, and software—all with a special emphasis on the Mouse. And with the new retail presence came a new monetary fixture: Disney Dollars, paper currency valid in the parks and stores, with none other than Mickey himself on the one-dollar bill. Within ten years, more than seven hundred Disney Stores opened throughout the world.

151

"The appeal of Mickey will continue, because if he hasn't reached a saturation point by now, he never will."—George Lucas

Mickey returned to the big screen in Mickey's Christmas Carol (1983). Mickey took on the sympathetic role of Bob Cratchit, and drew crowds to the theaters, as with the shorts of old.

152

Mickey's career stepped up with his theatrical comeback in the twenty-five-minute animated featurette *Mickey's Christmas Carol*, which premiered in England on October 20, 1983, and opened in America on December 16, 1983. Even though thirty years had passed since Mickey had last graced the screen, the true Hollywood star retained his youthful pluck. In truth, Donald's uncle, Scrooge McDuck, landed the starring role, but the film featured Mickey and Minnie as Mr. and Mrs. Bob Cratchit and offered Mickey an unusually poignant scene at the grave of Tiny Tim. The critically acclaimed film received an Academy Award nomination and soon became a television holiday perennial.

160

Fantasia's video success encouraged artists to restore more vitality to Mickey's character. "The tendency to make him too nice has limited him," said actor Wayne Allwine, voice of Mickey, in 1987. "We're going to try to direct him more toward Walt's version of Mickey, who was an actor. I think the character is still as Walt envisioned him: forever young and forever optimistic." As a result, in 1990 Mickey starred in a fast-paced featurette The Prince and the Pauper, which offered him two of his meatiest roles, with an unusually heavy amount of dialogue. Completely stepping out of his traditional role, Mickey next appeared in The Runaway Brain (1995). Needing money to buy Minnie an anniversary gift, Mickey gets mixed up with a mad doctor who switches Mickey's brain with that of a hulking Frankenstein's monster named Julius. Once the monster's brain is in Mickey's body, the World's Happiest Character mutates into a ragged, fanged, menacing wildmouse prowling the city streets, hunting for Minnie.

Mickey reverted back to his typical and reassuring self in 1999 with the home video entry, *Mickey's Once Upon a Christmas*, in which Mickey and Minnie enact a rendition of O. Henry's "The Gift of the Magi." That same year brought Mickey and friends to the small screen in their first-ever animated television series, *Mickey Mouse Works*. All-new cartoons featuring the "animated rat pack" (Mickey, Minnie, Goofy, Donald, Daisy, and Pluto) offered lively animation and fast-paced gags. Never before had the "sensational six" starred together in an original television series. Executive producers Roberts Gannaway and Tony Craig assembled the first full-time animation crew to produce original Mickey Mouse shorts since the Eisenhower era. Evergreen comic personalities Pluto, Goofy, and Donald made the transition easily. But animators took special care to develop a fuller personality for the woefully-neglected Daisy, a more self-reliant Minnie, and a less reverent Mickey, who for the first time in decades shows more of his true colors, becoming totally exasperated by Goofy's foolishness and going toe-to-toe with Donald when the duck loses control. Mickey also showed his old mettle as an adventurer. In one segment, he battles his old comic-strip foe, the Phantom Blot, and in "Mickey to The Rescue," he faces endless perils while trying to save Minnie from bizarre, Peg Leg Pete–devised deathtraps.

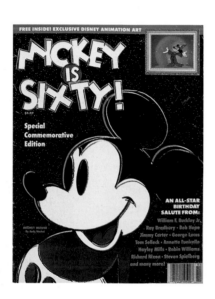

"Mouse and company are here for the long haul."

—*Hollywood Reporter* on Disney's *Mickey Mouse Works*, April 1999

ABOVE: *This special Commemorative Edition newsstand magazine, Mickey Is Sixty, from Time, Inc., featured notable artists and celebrities offering wisdom about the Mouse.*

LEFT & OPPOSITE: *At the end of the Millennium, one truth remained: Mickey Mouse loved Minnie Mouse. Their love affair has spanned seven decades, and they are still going strong.*

THE SHOW MUST GO ON

Despite his seventy-one years, Mickey had no plans to retire once the calendar turned to the year 2000; he remained as busy and as omnipresent as ever. Mickey Mouse had become more than the unspoken leader of Disney's stable of characters; his iconic image at its most basic level—three black circles—symbolized a corporate brand synonymous with Disney's values.

The release of *Fantasia/2000* made good on Walt's dream that his 1940 animated compilation would be perpetually reissued, its bill filled with ever-changing segments. Plans for *Fantasia/2000* included three highlights from *Fantasia*: "The Nutcracker Suite," "Dance of the Hours," and Mickey's episode, "The Sorcerer's Apprentice." But when time ran short, only Mickey's segment remained. The Mouse even found time to appear in a host sequence with Donald in which they, along with conductor James Levine, introduce "Pomp and Circumstance." The handshake between Mickey and famed-conductor Leopold Stokowski seen in *Fantasia* moved producer Don Hahn to extend the same courtesy to *Fantasia/2000*'s conductor. So, sixty years after the initial release of *Fantasia*, Mickey straightens Maestro Levine's tie.

OPPOSITE: *Mickey shakes the hand of conductor Leopold Stokowski during Fantasia (1940).*

BELOW OPPOSITE & BELOW: *Storyboards for the Fantasia/2000 host sequence in which Mickey interacts with conductor James Levine.*

"He's a universal symbol. He has a basic goodness, a niceness—well, a likable friendliness. It gets translated without the words." —Roy E. Disney, 1988

Mickey Mouse as a giant balloon wearing his Mouseketeer bandleader outfit and carrying a baton was the star of the Macy's November 23, 2000, seventy-fourth Thanksgiving Day Parade. Macy's Christmas-clad windows facing Broadway all featured Mickey, Minnie, and Pluto as three-dimensional molded moving sculptures in various outdoor and indoor holiday scenes. Inside the Art Deco main floor of Macy's, thousands of Mickey Mouse stuffed dolls, wearing the same red bandleader outfit, all sat on gift boxes wrapped in gold foil and tied with gold ribbon, ready to greet holiday shoppers. On every floor and in every department of New York's great department store, Mickey appeared as part of one kind of display or another; and expressly for the 2000 Christmas season, customers could purchase the limited-edition Mickey doll for $16.95 with any $35 purchase, or for $35 by itself. The association of Mickey Mouse and Macy's dates back to his first appearance as a giant balloon in the world-famous Thanksgiving Parade in 1935, and his return in 1970.

The following year, *Disney's House of Mouse*, a new series from Walt Disney Television Animation, premiered January 13, 2001, as part of the *Disney's One Saturday Morning* lineup, finally establishing Mickey Mouse's contemporary television presence. In the show, Mickey and Donald are co-owners of a Toontown-style nightclub whose audience consists entirely of Disney's classic animated characters. As Master of Ceremonies, Mickey introduces the cartoons, deals with meddling partner Donald, and tries to supervise the club's chaotic "live acts," such as the singing group The Big Bad Wolf and The Three Little Pigs, who literally bring the house down. Assorted Disney characters have new and unusual opportunities to interact. Of course, that leads to trouble when *The Lion King*'s Timon and Pumbaa eye Jiminy Cricket as a tasty snack, or *Hercules'* Pain and Panic act as bad influences on Pinocchio. The best of Mickey's character is back, but with a contemporary twist. He sports a fashionable wardrobe and is well aware of his celebrity status. As stakeholder in the club, Mickey relishes his position and will stop at nothing to protect his interests. For the Mouse, the show must go on.

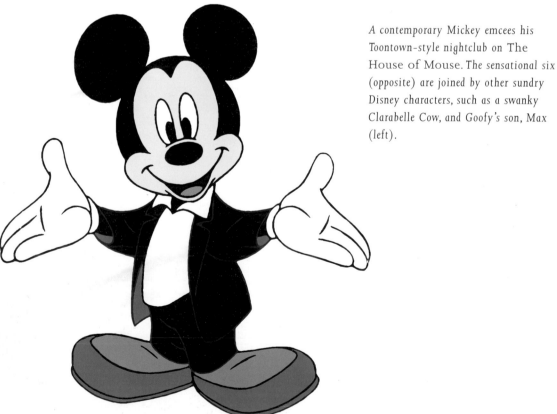

A contemporary Mickey emcees his Toontown-style nightclub on The House of Mouse. The sensational six (opposite) are joined by other sundry Disney characters, such as a swanky Clarabelle Cow, and Goofy's son, Max (left).

168

The Mickey Mysteries series, which was started in Europe, casts detectives Mickey and Minnie in a string of adventures.

Mickey Mouse jumped from the movie screen right onto the printed page with ease, building his following of fans across the world. *The Story of Mickey Mouse*, published in 1930 by Bibo and Lang and written by Bobette Bibo, the eleven-year-old daughter of the publisher, is the very first Mickey Mouse fiction. In this magazine format, Mickey, a.k.a. "Mouse Thirteen," falls down a chimney into the living room of lucky Walt Disney in Hollywood, U.S.A., who decides to turn the mischievous mouse into a movie star. After achieving

"Mickey's persistence s[p]

something timeless in the i[n]

in statu[

Touchdown Mickey, Mickey's Mechanical Man, Shanghaied, Mickey's Steamroller, and *Ye Olden Days.*

Whitman Publishing Company published numerous illustrated school readers and storybooks on Mickey Mouse and his friends. The company also produced Big Little Books usually available at the dime store for 10¢. For many children, these Big Little Books, generally 300 to 450 pages in length, were a first introduction to the novel form. Illustrations on every page connected the reader to the text and sometimes featured an action-flip page corner in

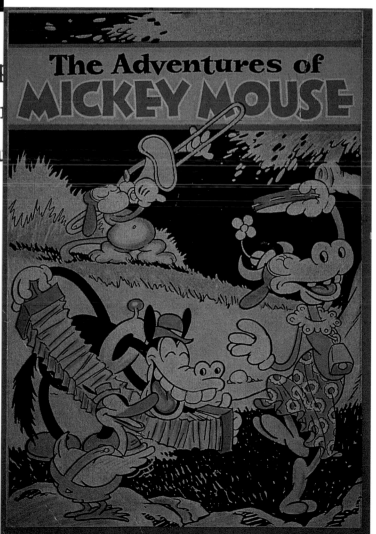

Hollywood stardom, Mickey and Minnie hobnob with the likes of Mary Pickford, Buddy Rogers, and Clara Bow at a movie opening. In one illustration, Mickey sings "My Mammy" before the cameras à la Al Jolson in *The Jazz Singer.*

Published in 1931, *The Adventures of Mickey Mouse* book #1 became the first of Mickey's early books to achieve large sales and distribution. The number-one book, profusely illustrated in color, soared to first place on best-seller lists for children and remained in print in hard and soft covers until World War II. In the story, Mickey is a barnyard rodent who lives "in a cozy nest under the floor of the old barn" not far from Minnie Mouse, who keeps a home safely

171

172

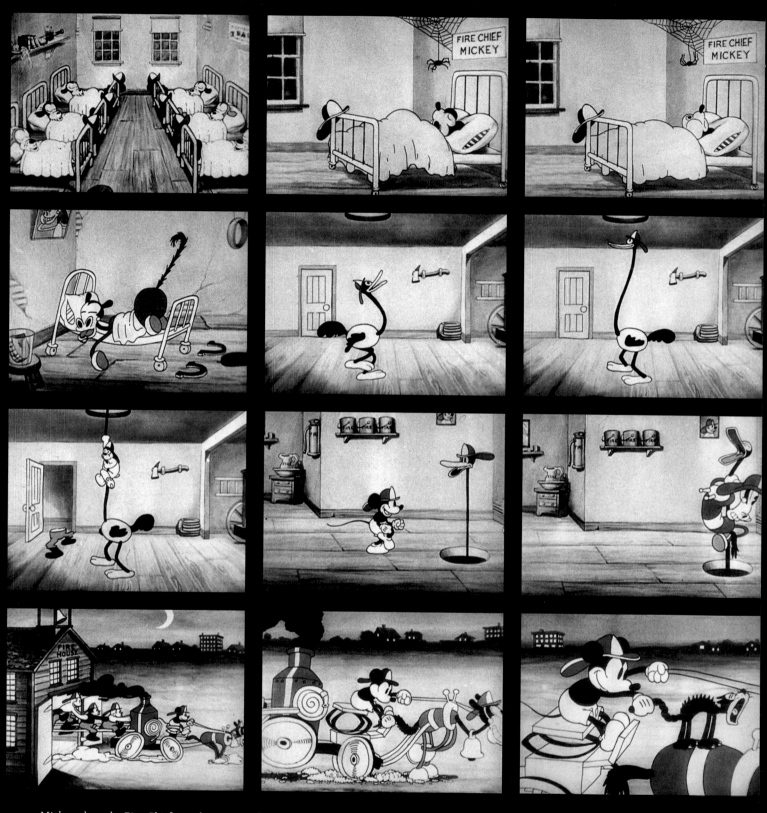

Mickey plays the Fire Chief in a harrowing adventure, The Fire Fighters (1930). An alarm sounds at the station house in the dead of night. The fire fighters race to the blaze that rages inside Minnie's apartment building. Ever the hero, Mickey saves Minnie from certain death.

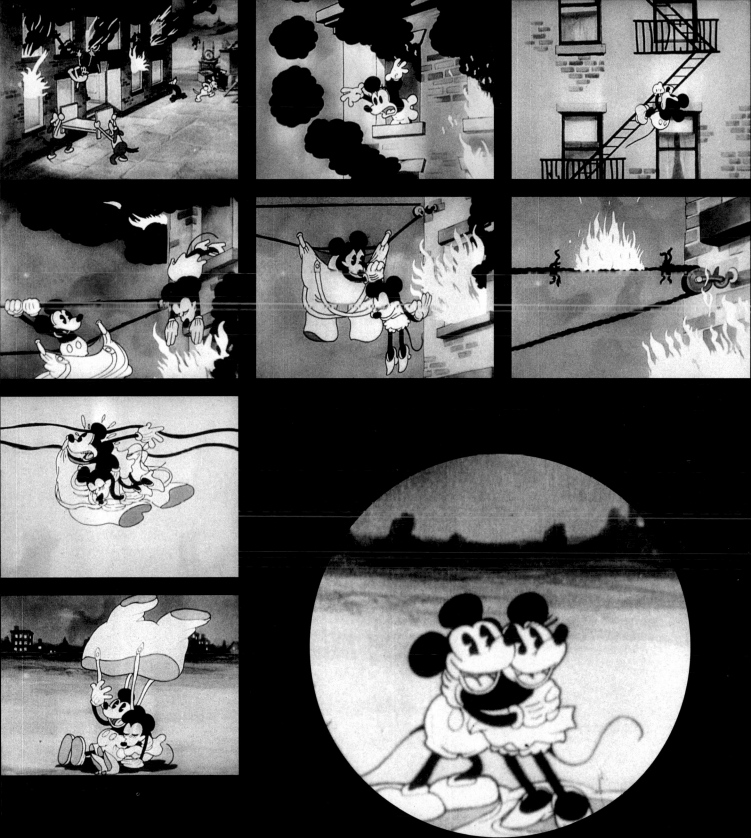

"Why Mickey? I like his attitude, which is no attitude. He's up for anything!"—Harmon Dresner

ABOVE: *Artist Ray Johnson's Mickey Mouse mail-art pen-and-ink drawing on an envelope*

OPPOSITE: *Mickey Mouse doll display at Mel Birnkrant's private residence, a converted nineteenth-century schoolhouse in upstate New York that houses his legendary vast collection of Mickey Mouse memorabilia*

Why do we love the Mouse?

Perhaps it's his personality. Mickey Mouse is upbeat in the face of adversity, never downtrodden or beaten by circumstance. In this sense he became a hero in the Depression, a role model during World War II, a friend to young Baby Boomers in the 1950s, a fashion statement in the 1960s, and a global icon ever since. He has been a wholesome, capable, brave, and determined young fellow who might take on the whole world if necessary. Never as violent as many of his cartoon colleagues, Mickey's intelligence has enabled him to be more resourceful and ingenious in the face of danger.

Often it is the uncomplicated spirit of good against all odds that helps Mickey win out and conquer in the end. Mickey may be a clever mouse, but he's never manipulative, bossy, or tyrannical. A sense of wonder and an open friendliness are at the core of his personality. Though he has been known to be a mischief-maker, he remains a contented and happy creature. Mickey approaches the world with compassion, energy, and a desire to have fun along the way.

177

RIGHT: *Mickey Mouse Halloween mask made of molded stiff cheesecloth, made by the Wornova Co., 1934*

OPPOSITE: *Litho on paper Mickey Mouse mask*

As an American Everyman, Mickey has worked at a variety of regular jobs with forthrightness and a go-getter attitude. Whether running a newspaper, solving a mystery, or looking for a lost treasure, Mickey gets the job done. *Mickey Mouse Will Not Quit!* is the title of a Wee Little Book, and to be sure, Mickey, with his self-confident spirit, has never been a quitter. Perhaps that's why audiences seem to have an instant rapport with him, feeling sympathetic toward his plight while being entertained by his humorous antics and mishaps along the way.

Perhaps it's his design that casts a spell over us. "Walt [Disney] felt there was something in the design of Mickey that would make babies always reach for the Mickey doll rather than other ones," animator Frank Thomas recalled. "A completeness, something made of circles." Many eminent artists and cartoonists today consider the early 1930s vintage Mickey Mouse to be the most perfectly developed abstract cartoon representation ever created. The rodent-like features, "pie-eyes," exaggerated long nose ending in a black

"For many years, as an adult, I searched for the Mickey Halloween mask. That face, that completely nuts look of fiery, intense animation—the smile, the eyes, the vividness of the characterization—is mind-boggling and still works so beautifully. I have the mask and I look at it now and get the same pleasure I did as a child. Friends come to my house, and it is bestrewn with these glaring Mickey Mouse–joy faces. I never get tired of seeing that face. It just gives me pleasure. What do friends think? Wisely, I never ask."—Maurice Sendak

RIGHT: *Bandleader Mickey introduces the show on the original Mickey Mouse Club on television.*

"I used to love watching *The Mickey Mouse Club* with Annette Funicello. Mickey Mouse would come on and say, 'Hi Folks!' and I'd think, Oh, boy! There's my friend, Mickey. I was inspired by how much energy went into the Mickey Mouse movies—it was really incredible to hear the voices, to see the drawings. It was quite fantastic and gave the illusion of 3-D in animation. It seemed that out of nowhere, Mickey had a bigger life than Walt Disney, has now outlived him, and is still going strong. That's pretty inspiring for a cartoon character." —Norm Rosenberger

ABOVE: *Illustration of Mickey and Minnie picnicking from a box cover of a Mickey Mouse puzzle game*

OPPOSITE: *Illustration of Mickey Mouse in sugar bowl from Mickey Mouse in Giant Land, hardcover book published in London by Collins, 1934*

stub, skinny black tail, short red pants, bulbous clownlike shoes, thick four-fingered gloves—this combination left an indelible imprint on the twentieth century, not to mention a legion of hardcore Mickey collectors. Many fans and collectors dismiss the later Mickeys, while others consider the early prototype rather crude. Especially in his revised, post-1939 design—with baggy long pants, larger head with infantile features, thickened snout, and rounded forehead—Mickey looks like one of his own comic-strip nephews, yet this version has its fans as well.

Mickey's love-appeal captivates babies, toddlers, and young children; and he continues to spark an immediate reaction from the "inner child" in adults. "He's my friend," says Judi Miller, best-selling mystery writer of *Save the Last Dance for Me* and *Hush, Little Baby.* "He always has been, since childhood. I trust him. Like me, he's up against the world—a survivor. He's nonthreatening—not an adult. He's spunky, perky. It's the ears ... the eyes! No, it's the smile. He's fun and he's bright."

181

"It's me! Mickey is me!"—Seven-year-old Jesse Tooker

So why do we love the Mouse? True, he was the first talking cartoon star, which ensures him a place in the history books, but not necessarily in our hearts. His design may be an aesthetically pleasing arrangement of circles, but so is that of many another durable and popular star. Neither is Mickey's sunny disposition unique: dozens of cartoon figures can claim it. Perhaps we never can fully explain why he continues to fascinate countless generations. That feeling is unique and timeless. So is Mickey Mouse.

BELOW: *"Sincerely Yours" Mickey Mouse button*

OPPOSITE: *Mickey and Minnie play with soap suds on the cardboard puzzle manufactured by the Vera Co., Paris, France.*

"This is tough, trying to explain Mickey. It's been done by experts and the best any of us has been able to come up with is the fact that Mickey is so simple and uncomplicated, so easy to understand, that you can't help liking him"—Walt Disney

182

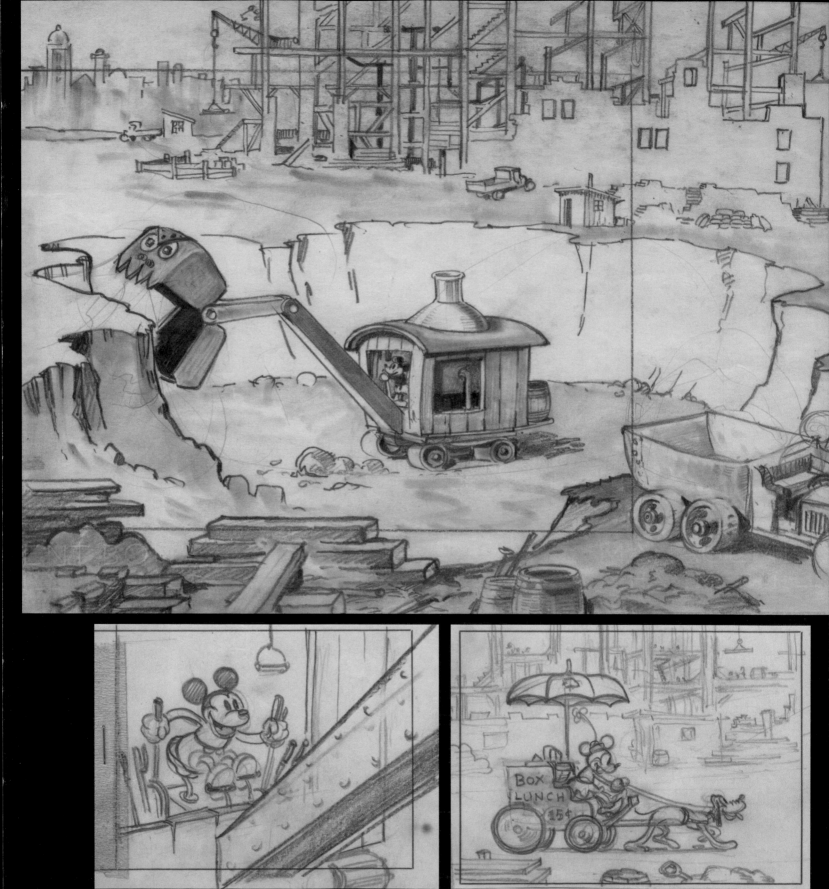

Mickey and his steam shovel: storyboards from
Building a Building (1933)

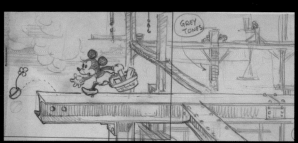

PHOTOGRAPHY/ILLUSTRATION CREDITS:
Page 1 courtesy Bertoia Auctions, the Wengel Collection; pages 3, 6, 11, 20 (gum card), 22 (button), 23, 30 (BLB), 31, 32, 33, 36, 38–39, 41, 44, 46–47, 48, 52, 53, 54, 56, 74–75, 77, 78, 79, 81 (matchbook), 82 (right), 83, 84, 86 (book illus.), 93 (left), 94 (button), 99, 102, 102 (wallet), 112–113, 115 (right), 119 (right), 120, 121, 123, 125, 126, 128, 129, 130–131, 132, 133, 134 (top right), 135, 142 (button), 145 (two right), 146, 147, 159 (bank detail), 162 (top), 170, 171, 172, 176, 178, 179, 182 and 183 by John Gilman; page 14 courtesy of the International Museum of Cartoon Art, Boca Raton, Florida; page 80 (gas mask) courtesy Tom Duncan; pages 82 (left), 119 (top), and 181 (left) courtesy Ted Hake; page 85 (all) by Philip Cohen; pages 115 (top right), 177, and endpapers courtesy Robert Heide collection; pages 115 and 117 from the Estate of Ray Johnson, courtesy Richard L. Feigen Gallery; page 116 courtesy John Fawcett; page 118 copyright © 2001 Andy Warhol Foundation for the Visual Arts/ARS, New York; page 127 Archives of Lincoln Center for the Performing Arts, Inc.; page 134 (John Gilman portrait and trouser leg) by David Schmidlapp; pages 148–149 copyright © Bettman/Corbis; page 155 (3 vintage greeting cards) courtesy Hallmark Cards; pages 156–157 copyright © Adrian Carroll; Eye Ubiquitous/Corbis; page 161 (car) by Stephen Douglas Hooper; and pages 166–167 courtesy of Macy's Photo Archives

ACKNOWLEDGMENTS

AT DISNEY: Thank you to Disney Editions Editorial Director Wendy Lefkon for her vision and encouragement; to Senior Editor Sara Baysinger who guided this book from the very beginning idea stage to the finished result; to Jody Revenson for being on the spot and ready to help; and to Monica Mayper, Christopher Caines, and Jaime Herbeck for dotting our i's and crossing our t's. Thank you to Dave Smith and Robert Tieman at the Disney Archives in Burbank. To "official" portrait artist and Imagineer John Hench for sharing his vast first-hand knowledge of Mickey's history from "The Sorcerer's Apprentice" to current plans for redesigning the walk-around characters. And to Peggy Van Pelt, whose invaluable insight helped to shape the spirit and tone of the narrative.

AT WELCOME ENTERPRISES, INC: Thank you to Clark Wakabayashi, whose contribution was invaluable; to Jon Glick for his masterful design; and to Jacinta O'Halloran for her research and stewardship of the project.

SPECIAL ACKNOWLEDGMENTS: Thanks to Mel Birnkrant and Harmon Dresner for opening up their private Mickey Mouse collections.

ALSO THANKS TO: Michael Malce, Mary Lou Dettmer, Charmaine Chester, Bill Wilson, 'Hoop' a.k.a. Stephen Douglas Hooper, and his mother Bea; George and Ann Harris, Heidi Gilman and Frank Wajnarowitz and Claire-Sarah and Marina, Joe, Eloise and Montana Damone; Sam Lieber, Quinn Kelly, Cali Coulter, James Fitzgerald, Jr., Jerry Pagano, Brian Walker, Stephen Charla at the International Museum of Cartoon Art in Boca Raton, Carol Tooker and family; Madeline, Sam, Jess, Brad, Lauren and Emma Violet Hoffer, Doris Dinger, Philip Cohen, Henry Mazzeo, Zac Zimmerman, Jerry Lee, Miwako Nishizawa, Adam Fisher, Alice Wong, Robert Lesser, Eunice Birnkrant, Kenneth Anger, Nancy Keller, Steve Gould, Peter Gilman, Laura Gilman, Suzy Hibbard, David Schmidlapp, Tomi Ungerer, Seth Weine, Tom Duncan, Edward Albee (born in 1928—the same year as Mickey Mouse), Victor Bockris, John Fawcett, Louisa McCune, Michelle Maiullo, Judi Miller, Jeremiah Newton, Kelly Crow, Bonnie Slotnick Cookbooks in Greenwich Village, the Heitke family in California, Ava Cammarano, Maris and Mireille Hanson, and Kojin and Kai Glick.

FOR THEIR CONTRIBUTION TO THIS BOOK:
Ted Hake of Hake's Americana and collectibles, P.O. Box 1444, York, PA 17405 www.hakes.com

The Estate of Ray Johnson

Richard L. Feigen & Co. Gallery

Bob Rutan, annual events, Macy's Department Store, New York

Rachel Bolton and Sharmon Robertson at Hallmark Cards and the Hallmark Archives

Bill Bertoia of Bertoia Auctions in Vineland, New Jersey

Philip Cohen Photographics, 41 Yosemite Avenue, Oakland, CA 946

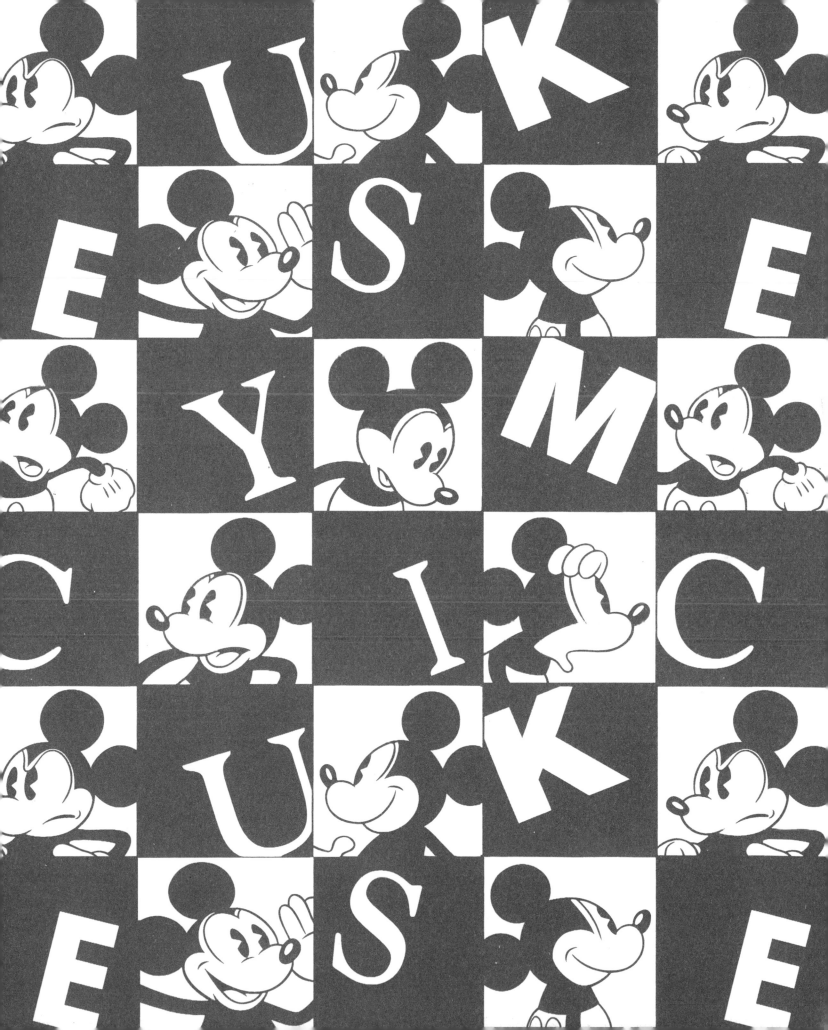